Portraits in Black

by
Doris Hunter Metcalf

illustrated by Paul Manktelow

Cover by Paul Manktelow

Copyright © Good Apple, Inc., 1990

ISBN No. 0-86653-531-4

Printing No. 987

Good Apple, Inc.
1204 Buchanan, Box 299
Carthage, IL 62321-0299

Table of Contents

GA1147

GA1147

Dedication

This book is dedicated to all who want to learn
and know of the achievements
of black Americans.

To my husband, Weston,
for his support and encouragement.
To my sons
Rockell, Kendric, and Sevante.

Introduction

No study of American history is complete without a study of the contributions and achievements of black Americans. From the earliest existence of this country to the present time, Blacks have played a major role in its development and progress. Despite barriers set before them, Blacks have managed to develop their talents to make contributions in all areas of American life. However, many of their contributions and achievements have not been given proper credit and recognition.

Most textbooks and social studies programs do not include enough information about Blacks and other minorities.

This book is designed to supplement textbook and social studies programs. It contains twelve units of information that present Blacks as inventors, scientists, doctors, lawyers and judges, educators, artists, leaders, cowboys, pioneers, politicians, writers, explorers and settlers.

Each unit contains background information, biographies and related activity sheets.

These units can be used in a learning center setting to provide meaningful learning experiences for those students who finish regular classroom work early. They can be used by individual students as independent study projects or by the entire class as supplementary learning activities.

The study of the achievements of black Americans can add a new dimension to the study of American history. It can build a positive relationship between Blacks and other students, and it can provide an opportunity for all students to learn about and appreciate another group of people who helped to make this country great. It is hoped that these units of study will stimulate students to go further and explore deeper the contributions and achievements of other black Americans.

GA1147

The Father of Black History
Dr. Carter G. Woodson
(1875-1950)

If you have ever studied about black Americans during one of your history lessons in school, then perhaps you have studied some of the works of Dr. Carter G. Woodson. Dr. Woodson devoted much of his life to studying and writing the history of black Americans.

Dr. Woodson was born in New Canton, Virginia, in 1875. His parents were poor; they could not afford to send him to school regularly. When he was seventeen, he earned money for his education by working in the coal mine. This was a slow way to earn his education, but Dr. Woodson was determined to get an education. He was twenty-two years old when he graduated from high school. Most people have graduated from college by the time they reach twenty-two.

Dr. Woodson earned a teaching degree from Berea College in Kentucky and taught school in Virginia. During summers, he studied at the University of Chicago. He spent one year studying in Asia and Europe including one half year at the Sorbonne, a university in France.

Later, he attended Harvard and graduated in 1912 with a Ph.D. degree. Three years later he organized the Association for the Study of Negro Life and History. The name of the organization has now been changed to the Association for the Study of Afro-American Life and History (ASALH). He believed that black Americans were a part of America and that their history and life were important enough to be studied. Dr. Woodson had three main reasons for forming the ASALH: 1. He wanted people to learn to appreciate the life and history of black Americans. 2. He wanted people to better understand black people. 3. He wanted black Americans to have hope for a brighter future.

Today, the ASALH produces study kits to help students in schools and colleges learn more about black Americans.

In 1926 Dr. Woodson began the observance of Black History Week. This was a week designed to focus on the achievements of black Americans. He chose the week in February with the birth dates of two great Americans, Abraham Lincoln and Frederick Douglass. Today, the entire month of February is observed as Black History Month. During this month many programs and activities are planned to honor the contributions and achievements of black Americans.

Because of his dedication to the study and life of black Americans, Dr. Woodson is called The Father of Black History.

Dr. Woodson led a full and useful life. His studying, writing and speeches kept him busy. On April 3, 1950, Dr. Woodson's life came to an end.

Every February as thousands of black Americans celebrate Black History Month, they remember the man who started it all—Dr. Carter Goodwin Woodson.

GA1147

Woodson's Puzzle

Use the words in the word bank to complete the puzzle. Unscramble the circled letters to reveal two important words.

Word Bank

Sorbonne February Carter Canton Berea on twenty-two year black Harvard life coal

1. He studied at ⃝ ___ ___ ___ ___ College in Kentucky.

2. He completed high school at age ⃝ ___ ___ ___ ___ ___ - ___ ___ ___.

3. His first name was ___ ⃝ ___ ___ ___ ___.

4. He worked in the ___ ___ ___ ⃝ mines to finance his education.

5. He studied for one ___ ___ ___ ⃝ in Europe.

6. He studied at the ⃝ ___ ___ ___ ___ ___ ___ ___ in France.

7. ___ ___ ___ ___ ⃝ history is the study of black Americans.

8. He was born in New ⃝ ___ ___ ___ ___ ___, Virginia.

9. He earned a Ph.D. degree at ⃝ ___ ___ ___ ___ ___ ___.

10. He died ⃝ ___ April 3, 1950.

11. He had a full and useful ___ ⃝ ___ ___.

12. ___ ___ ___ ___ ___ ___ ⃝ is Black History Month.

Two important words:

___ ___ ___ ___ ___ ___ ___ ___ ___ ___ ___ ___ ___ ___ ___ ___ ___

GA1147

Celebration Time

Choose a month for a particular celebration.

Give the name of the month. _____

_____

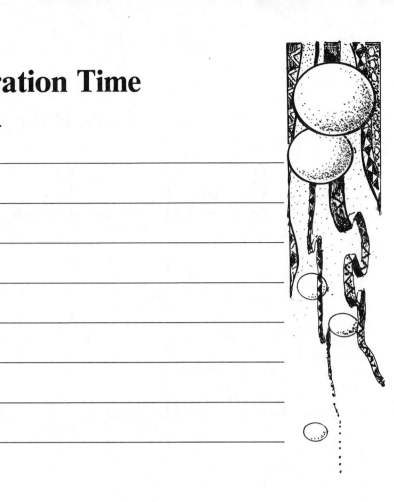

Give the name of the event to be celebrated. _____

_____

_____

Tell how the month will be celebrated. _____

_____

_____

Write activities for the celebration here.

1. _____

_____

2. _____

_____

3. _____

_____

4. _____

_____

GA1147

February

Black History Month

	1 Langston Hughes, poet born in 1902.	**2** In 1865 John S. Rock became the first black lawyer to practice before the U.S. Supreme Court.	**3** In 1794 slavery was abolished in all of France and her colonies.	**4** Thomas Peterson, first Black to exercise right to vote under the 15th Amendment died in New Jersey.	**5** Rev. C.T. Walker, famous minister, Tabernacle Baptist Church, Augusta, GA, was born in 1858.	**6** 10,000 Blacks demonstrated against lynching and racial discrimination in New York City in 1917.
7 In 1966 Emmett Ashford became the first black umpire in the major league.	**8** In 1951 Pvt. Edward Cleaborn of the U.S. Army was awarded the Distinguished Service Cross.	**9** Outstanding poet Paul Lawrence Dunbar died in 1906.	**10** Birthday of Leontyne Price, one of the world's greatest soprano singers.	**11** In 1837 Vermont asked Congress to abolish slavery in the District of Columbia.	**12** In 1909 a group of Blacks and Whites met at Niagara Falls to begin to organize the NAACP.	**13** In 1874 J.T. Carter, lawyer and insurance company President, was born.
14 Frederick Douglass, orator, statesman and abolitionist, was born on this date.	**15** In 1946 Cornelius Johnson, 1936 Olympic high jump champion, died at the age of 32.	**16** George Young, Missionary to Africa and Ame Church bishop, died in 1949.	**17** A.C. Richardson invented a churn in 1891.	**18** Famous architect, Paul Revere Williams, was born in 1894.	**19** Henry Eubanks, three-term member of the Ohio Legislature, died in 1913 at the age of 55.	**20** Birthday of Sidney Poitier, first black man to win an Oscar for best actor in *Lilies of the Field*.
21 Militant black leader, Malcolm X, was shot to death in New York in 1965.	**22** In 1975 Henry (Hank) Aaron received the Spingarn Medal for achievements in baseball.	**23** Dr. W.E.B. Du Bois, educator, writer and scholar, was born in Massachusetts in 1868.	**24** D.A. Payne, Ame Church bishop, was born in 1811.	**25** In 1870 Hiram Revels took the oath of office to become the first black U.S. senator.	**26** In 1869 the 15th Amendment concerning black suffrage was passed.	**27** Marian Anderson, concert artist, was born in 1902.
28 Famous lady poet, Phillis Wheatley visited President George Washington on her birthday in 1776.	**29** LEAP YEAR					

4

Calendar Personalities

Select the names and dates of five persons from the black history calendar that interest you.

1. List their names and achievements in the space below.

Name   **Achievement**

A. _____   _____

B. _____   _____

C. _____   _____

D. _____   _____

E. _____   _____

2. Research additional information about one of the calendar persons and make an interesting report to the class.

3. Design an award to be presented to a calendar person for his/her achievement.

4. Write a letter to a calendar person inviting him/her to visit your hometown. Tell him/her why you think that your hometown is a good place to visit.

5. Write a poem to a calendar person.

GA1147

Black Educators

Can you imagine a society where children were not allowed to learn to read or write? During the early years of slavery, black children were not allowed to learn to read or write. In the South, laws were passed so that anyone who taught black children to read were dealt with harshly. Despite these laws some Blacks still managed to learn; some were taught secretly. Others were taught by their masters so that they could be of better use to them.

During the 1700's, a few schools for Blacks were opened by religious groups and individuals who wanted to help educate black children. When the cotton gin was invented in 1893, there was no hope for more black schools in the South. The gin made it possible for large amounts of cotton to be processed. The more cotton that was picked from the fields and processed at the gin, the more money that it would bring for plantation owners. Therefore black children were forced to work long hours beside their parents in the cotton fields. There was no time for them to learn, and there was no one to teach them.

In 1831 another incident happened that put education out of the reach of black children. It was called the Nat Turner Rebellion. Nat Turner was a slave who had learned to read and write. He believed that he was sent by God to deliver his people from slavery. One night Turner and his friends armed themselves and killed Turner's master and his master's family. After the rebellion, many plantation owners feared that if Blacks were taught to read and write, they would grow up and rebel just as Nat Turner did.

After the Civil War when slaves were freed, the federal government set up the Freedmen's Bureau. This agency helped set up schools for former slaves and their children. Many black children took advantage of the opportunity to learn to read and write. Some of the schools that the Bureau opened became outstanding black colleges such as Atlanta University, Hampton Institute in Virginia, and Howard University in Washington, D.C.

In the 1800's and 1900's several black educators who had received an education themselves, set out to help other Blacks. Some wrote books, some spoke out for better education and others started schools of their own.

The Miller Brewing Company of Milwaukee selected the following black educators for its Gallery of Greats 1988 calendar series. They represent the thousands of black educators who have made great contributions in the field of education.

1. Carter G. Woodson—New Canton, Virginia
2. Mary Frances Berry—Nashville, Tennessee
3. George McKenna—New Orleans, Louisiana
4. Nolen Ellison—Kansas City, Kansas
5. Alain Locke—Philadelphia, Pennsylvania
6. W.E.B. Du Bois—Great Barrington, Massachusetts
7. John Hope Franklin—Rentiesville, Oklahoma
8. Clifton Wharton, Jr.—Boston, Massachusetts
9. Quiester Craig—Montgomery, Alabama
10. Erma Chansler Johnson—Texas
11. Wilson Riles—Louisiana
12. Ida Daniel Dark—Pennsylvania

GA1147

Native States

1. Locate the native state of each Gallery of Greats educator.

2. Place the number of each educator in the correct state.

3. Select one of the educators and write a biographical paragraph about him/her.

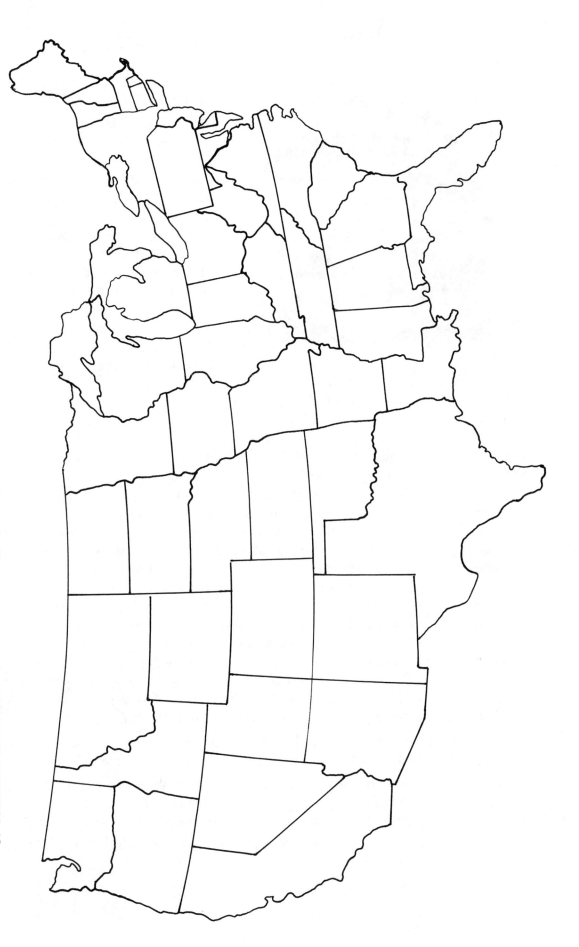

GA1147

Mary McLeod Bethune

In the city of Daytona Beach, Florida, stands a college that was founded by a courageous black woman who sold sweet potato pies and cakes to help finance her school for black children. That courageous woman was Mary McLeod Bethune. She was born on a farm in Mayesville, South Carolina, in 1875. Her parents were free but poor. At the age of eleven, she learned to read. This was a big accomplishment for a poor black girl in those days. Education was expensive but Mary's parents felt that she had a special talent. They looked for a way to send her to school. When a small school opened near her home, Mary enrolled, but she soon learned all that the little school could teach her. She went back to the farm to help in the cotton fields. Mary was determined to get an education. She was certain that someday she would get an opportunity to further her education. The opportunity finally came. A Quaker teacher offered to pay for the education of one well-deserving black girl. Mary was selected as that well-deserving girl. She attended Scotia Seminary in North Carolina and Moody Bible Institute in Chicago. After graduation, she went to teach at Haines Institute in Augusta, Georgia. Mary had educated herself, and she wanted to share her education with others. When she heard that railroads were to be constructed along the east coast of Florida, she thought of all the black families who would come to work on those railroads, and she thought of all the poor black children who would not be able to afford an education. Mary had learned that getting an education was an almost impossible task for poor black children. She remembered how hard it was for her. With $1.50, courage, determination and faith, she set out to build a school. She began with an old building near the city dump in Daytona Beach, Florida. Crates and boxes were used for chairs and desks. To finance her school, she wrote articles, contacted churches, clubs and civic organizations for donations and sold sweet potato pies and cakes. Her school for five little girls grew to become Bethune College. In 1923 Bethune College merged with Cookman Institute to become Bethune-Cookman College that is now an outstanding four-year college. In 1935 Mary McLeod Bethune received the NAACP Spingarn Medal for outstanding achievements. That same year, she founded the National Council of Negro Women.

Presidents Calvin Coolidge, Herbert Hoover, Franklin Roosevelt and Harry Truman appointed Mrs. Bethune to various government positions during their administrations.

In 1974 a national memorial was erected in her honor in Washington, D.C. In March of 1985, the Mary McLeod Bethune commemorative postage stamp was issued in her honor. Her last homesite in Washington, D.C., is now the Bethune Museum Archives.

Mary McLeod Bethune died in 1955. She had devoted her entire life to the improvement of educational opportunities for Blacks.

GA1147

Extra! Extra! Read All About It!

You are a newspaper reporter for the *Daily Gazette Times*. Read the Mary McLeod Bethune story and write a headline and news story for your newspaper.

Be sure to include the five W's.

Who

What

When

Where

Why

GA1147

Black Lawyers and Judges

Do you like to express your opinion on different issues? Do you like to present your ideas to others? Do you like to help make decisions? If you enjoy doing these things, perhaps you would make a good lawyer or judge someday. Lawyers and judges are very important people. Many black lawyers and judges serve in the judicial system of this nation. Every day, hundreds of black lawyers argue their cases before the bar or sit on the bench to hear these cases.

During the twentieth century, the best talents and brains in the legal profession have focused on civil rights. Top rated black lawyers such as William Hart, James Cobb, Herman Moore, William Hastie, Charles Houston and many others have helped move this country closer to freedom and equality for black Americans.

Spottswood Robinson, Raymond Alexander of Philadelphia, A.T. Walden of Atlanta, Robert Ming of Chicago, Henry Richardson of Indianapolis, Pery Howard of Washington, D.C., and Arthur Shores of Birmingham have all served with distinction and honor.

The field of black lawyers and judges is not limited to men only. Many talented and bright black women serve in this profession as well. Charlotte Ray was the first black woman lawyer in the United States. She graduated from Howard University in 1872.

Jabe Bolan became the first black woman judge in the United States. Constance Motley was first to become judge of a federal district court. Jewel Lafontant was first to become a United States assistant district attorney.

Each day the number of black women entering the law profession continues to grow. Three black judges took the lead in becoming outstanding figures on the bench: William Hastie, James Parson, and Thurgood Marshall.

The most famous of the three and the one most often remembered during the civil rights era is Thurgood Marshall. His valiant fight for equality and justice for Blacks earned him the title "Mr. Civil Rights." One of his most famous cases was the 1954 desegregation case in which separate schools for black and white children were ruled unconstitutional. In 1961 Marshall was appointed to the United States Court of Appeals and solicitor general of the United States. In 1967 he reached the uppermost level in the justice system. Thurgood Marshall was appointed associate justice of the United States Supreme Court. To become a supreme court justice is the dream of many lawyers and judges. Only a few are chosen for this great honor. For Thurgood Marshall the dream had become a reality.

GA1147

Evidence

To prepare his/her case, a lawyer must have evidence.

Look for evidence of fifteen black lawyers in the puzzle below. The last names may appear up, down, across, backwards or diagonally.

Here are the words to look for:

Alexander   Clemon
Cobb   Hart
Hastie   Howard
Marshall   Ming
Moore   Parson
Richardson   Robinson
Shores   Walden
Wilson

```
I H A O Q M V U P A M V Y I G Q Y W E A A T L I H
H N I A T S R K B V H T K H O R F Q S C E P D N P
B T A I Q L A V H H P K O P W Y T N V V X J O W L
R O D O J M N X C L W S O D T T Q T Y Q L S U X R
K J I O O A W G L M U H W E E M X Y R T D P P C I
O A A O X D V A O M T O O A W K A P Y R A I Q W N
E R R T F H G E L Q N R K V U P C L A A S Z Q A Z
C E M Q O T L B U D E E R J A X Z H L H A A J Q H
G L I C E X K L H D E S J B N S C L B A U K K R U
A X P I G D O C N O M N J F P I Z J U I H W Z F O
E E F C O Q I A O V I X Z T R T M B M B T S H Q I
F U G W R P X N P B H C S X I W F Q X Q W R R S J
U Y L N L E O I T P B U Q V Y M Q W Q N V N C A S
D Z N J L S J U R G H W J S E S H N I X Q S H W M
R U R A R V U H V A Z Y R F G Z E G K L U W S Z N
A I O A S S F V S V T U E P W G J Q N O S M U O J
W F P I B H T T C V B H E D K G L A P V R O S X U
O R K V Q H I C O R L E X C Q Z U M E Y Y N N N U
H D X E A E T Q V D Q K U J A X U P Q C I R S K R
M Q V W C O C V U W B Y V B N I M C I B Q N N U P
Y J R N F E D F R C L I W D A D Y X O B Z W T I L
S Y N O M E L C N Q E I W A F N U R L U G M I N G
G B A E M L I X Y G W W C A G B G F I O O B W G I
M O U J V E K P C D M N M K H F S S V F L H C R A
P V U A W P F C Y U E Q C I U O Y W L B O Y I V A
```

GA1147

The Margaret Bush Wilson Story

On January 13, 1975, a St. Louis lawyer gained national fame when she was elected President of the National Board of Directors of the NAACP—National Association for the Advancement of Colored People. Margaret Bush Wilson became the first black woman ever to hold such a position in the NAACP since it was founded in 1909. After the election, she appeared on such national television shows as *Meet the Press, The David Susskind Show, A.M. America* and *The Today Show.* Success for Margaret Bush Wilson did not come overnight. It was the results of determination, patience and dedication to her work. Her achievements came a few years at a time. Each step put her closer to her goal of serving her people.

Margaret Bush Wilson was born into a prominent middle class family in St. Louis, Missouri. She graduated from high school with honors and enrolled in college at Talladega, a private, black college in east Alabama. Her father wanted her to become a teacher or nurse, but Margaret Bush Wilson had something else in mind. She wanted to become a lawyer. With her goal in mind, she entered Lincoln University School of Law in St. Louis and graduated in 1943. After her admission to the Missouri Bar, she began a law firm in St. Louis.

From 1943-1945 she served as United States Attorney in the United States Department of Agriculture.

In 1948 she became the first black woman to run for congress in the state of Missouri.

Ten years laters, she became the first black woman president of the St. Louis NAACP.

From 1961-1962 she was an Assistant Attorney General of the state of Missouri.

In 1965 she served as a Legal Service Specialist in President Johnson's War on Poverty Program.

Her accomplishments are many, but her greatest was her position on the National Board of Directors of the NAACP from 1975-1984. This was a most important position. Here, she helped to make decisions for one of the largest civil rights organizations in the nation.

Margaret Bush Wilson still lives in the neighborhood where she grew up, now located in the black ghetto in St. Louis. She wants to remain among her people so that she might stay in touch with their problems. She says that her ghetto neighborhood is a "swinging place." "I have marvelous neighbors, I'm only five minutes from the symphony, ten minutes from the art gallery and fifteen minutes from the ball park," she says.

Attorney Wilson has many symbols of her accomplishments. The walls of her office are adorned with many plaques, awards and certificates from many prominent groups, organizations and individuals. She pays little attention to them as she goes about her daily tasks of helping her people.

Margaret's Pearl

A pearl is formed inside an oyster shell when a tiny sand grain or other foreign object enters its body. The sand grain is covered layer after layer until it forms a beautiful pearl.

Below is a pearl representing the achievements of attorney Margaret Bush Wilson. Place an achievement inside each dated layer to show how she became a shining pearl in the legal profession.

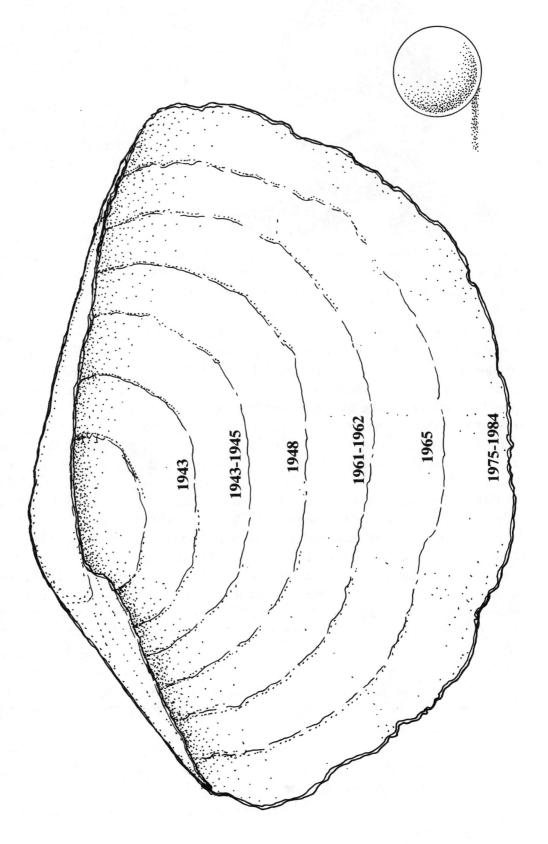

1943

1943-1945

1948

1961-1962

1965

1975-1984

13

The U.W. Clemon Story

In 1941 Mose Clemon, a Mississippi sharecropper moved his wife and nine children to Birmingham, Alabama, to work in the steel mill. One of those nine children was U.W. Clemon, now a federal judge in the state of Alabama.

As U.W. began to grow up, he observed the unfair treatment of black people firsthand. It was happening right in his own family. His dad Mose had worked twenty-eight years as a bricklayer's helper. Even though his work was as good as the rest of the bricklayers, he could not get a promotion or an increase in salary. His father Mose died in 1969. Three years later, U.W. became one of the lawyers who filed a discrimination suit against the steel mill company. As a result, unfair promotion practices were discontinued at the steel mill. Judge Clemon calls this case one that gave him great pleasure and one that he was proud to be a part of.

When he was growing up, U.W. was a determined and bold youngster always speaking out for what he felt was right. When he graduated from Westfield High in Birmingham, he enrolled at Morehouse College in Atlanta in the fall of 1961. (1) He later dropped out because of physical education requirements. The late great scholar and educator, Dr. Benjamin Mays, expressed sadness over Clemon's choice. He had seen something good in U.W., and he wanted to see him succeed. U.W. returned to Birmingham and enrolled in Miles College. While attending Miles he was a very active student. He was editor of the student newspaper, president of the student government and later valedictorian of his class. He became involved in the Civil Rights Movement and worked under the leadership of Dr. Martin Luther King, helping to organize boycotts of downtown stores in Birmingham. (2) When he was a nineteen-year-old college freshmen, he appeared before an all white city council in Birmingham to protest racial city ordinances. This was a bold act for a young black man. He was told to "Get out of town by sundown." U.W. was disappointed and angry, but he would not let this stop him from fighting for what he felt was right. (3) Once he was ordered from a downtown Birmingham department store at gunpoint because he drank from a water fountain with a sign that said "white only." Each unfair act seemed to challenge and inspire him toward his goal. He wanted to become a lawyer. Not just any lawyer, but a civil rights lawyer, one who would fight against injustices such as the ones he had experienced.

With this goal in mind, he entered law school at Columbia University in New York. Again he became a dropout, but he soon returned and in 1968 he graduated from Columbia Law School with honors. After graduation, he returned to Birmingham, joined a law firm and began practicing law. In 1974 U.W. was elected to the Alabama Senate becoming one of the first Blacks to serve in the Upper House.

His achievements and contributions were many, but his greatest accomplishment came on July 3, 1980. His nomination by President Jimmy Carter was approved by the Senate, and he became the first black federal judge in the state of Alabama.

When asked about his position as Alabama's first black federal judge, Clemon simply says "It's a very real challenge."

Judge Clemon does not want to be remembered for being the first black federal judge in the state of Alabama. Instead, he wants to be remembered for having done a job well and for his fair and equal treatment of all people.

GA1147

Clemon's Lemonade

Have you ever heard the saying: "If life gives you a lemon, make lemonade"?

This saying illustrated the life of Judge U.W. Clemon. When he met with obstacles, he worked to overcome them and turned them into something good.

List an obstacle or problem in each lemon. (Hint): Look for the numbered sentences in the story.

Write the achievements of Judge Clemon in each pitcher of lemonade.

1968   1974   1980

15

GA1147

Your Story

The year is 2019. You have become a famous person. Tell your story.

How old are you now?

What famous thing(s) have you done?

Did you have to overcome any problems in order to become famous?

If so, what were they?

Begin with the date of your birth and list important things that you have achieved so far in your life.

Include things such as trophies, awards, certificates and other honors.

16

David Walker and Sojourner Truth

During the many years of struggle for freedom and equality, many black leaders gave their lives to help make America a better place for Blacks to live. David Walker was one such leader. He was born a free man in North Carolina in 1785, but he wanted freedom for all people of his race. In 1827 he settled in Boston and became a leader in the Boston Colored Association. This organization worked against slavery. He also wrote and helped distribute the first black newspaper in the United States, *Freedom's Journal.* In 1829

he published a booklet called *An Appeal to the Colored Citizens of the World.* His booklet was later called *Appeal.* In the booklet, he urged black slaves to get an education and to use force if necessary to gain their freedom. Shortly after it was published, slave owners became angry. They did not want anyone to tell their slaves to fight for their freedom. Soon afterwards David Walker died mysteriously. Many people believed that he was murdered.

Many early leaders traveled across the country to speak out against slavery. They were called abolitionists. Sojourner Truth was one of the best-known abolitionists of her time. She was the first black woman to speak out against slavery. She was born a slave in New York but was freed in 1828 under a New York law that forbade slavery. Her name at first was Isabella Baumfree, but she changed it to Sojourner Truth when she felt that God had called her to preach. Her new name meant "traveler for truth." She began making speeches about God and his love, and then she began making speeches about the abolition of slavery. She began to travel throughout New England and the Midwest speaking out against slavery. She was one of the most dramatic speakers of all times. Whenever she spoke, she stunned her audience with her deep voice and her quick wit. In 1864, she went to Washington, D.C., where she visited President Lincoln in the White House and helped improve living conditions for Blacks who lived there. She also helped to find jobs and homes for slaves who had escaped from the South.

GA1147

Your Appeal

David Walker's *Appeal* urged slaves to fight for their freedom. Select one of the topics below and write an appeal telling how you feel about the topic and try to make others feel the way you do.

Topics

Peace
Equal Rights
Justice
Clean Air
Nuclear Energy

_____ 's Appeal
(your name)

_____
(name of topic)

Sojourner's Truth

Place a check (✓) beside the true statements about Sojourner Truth. Place an (x) beside the false statements and rewrite the false statements to make them true.

_____ 1. Sojourner Truth was the first black woman to speak out against slavery.

_____ 2. She was born in 1897.

_____ 3. Her name Sojourner Truth meant "a journey to the future."

_____ 4. She visited President Lincoln in the White House.

_____ 5. She changed her name from Sojourner Truth to Isabella Baumfree.

GA1147

Harriet Tubman

Several black leaders became famous as "conductors" on the Underground Railroad. The Underground Railroad was not a railroad at all. It was a network of hiding places to help slaves escape to the North. The "conductors" led the slaves from one hiding place to another. These hiding places were sometimes called stations.

William Still and David Ruggles were conductors, but the most famous conductor of them all was Harriet Tubman. Harriet Tubman was born a slave in 1821 in the state of Maryland. At the age of twenty-five, she escaped to the North. Between 1850 and 1860, she made nineteen trips to the South and secretly led over 300 slaves to freedom. She became known as The Black Moses of her people.

Being a conductor on the Underground Railroad involved great danger and hardship especially for a black woman. Harriet could lose her life or be captured and enslaved again. But freedom for the slaves was of great importance to Harriet. A reward of $40,000 dollars was once offered for her capture. But no one could capture Harriet. She did not have the opportunity to learn to read or write, but she was clever enough to outwit her most hostile enemies.

During the Civil War, Harriet served as a nurse and spy for the Union. When she died in 1913 she was buried in Ohio with military honors.

Directions:

Use the numbered alphabet to break the code and reveal an interesting fact about Harriet Tubman.

Code:

1 = A, 2 = B, 3 = C, 4 = D, 5 = E, 6 = F, 7 = G, 8 = H, 9 = I, 10 = J, 11 = K, 12 = L, 13 = M, 14 = N, 15 = O, 16 = P, 17 = Q, 18 = R, 19 = S, 20 = T, 21 = U, 22 = V, 23 = W, 24 = X, 25 = Y, 26 = Z

$\overline{8}$ $\overline{1}$ $\overline{18}$ $\overline{18}$ $\overline{9}$ $\overline{5}$ $\overline{20}$ $\overline{20}$ $\overline{21}$ $\overline{2}$ $\overline{13}$ $\overline{1}$ $\overline{14}$

$\overline{23}$ $\overline{1}$ $\overline{19}$ $\overline{1}$ $\overline{3}$ $\overline{15}$ $\overline{14}$ $\overline{4}$ $\overline{21}$ $\overline{3}$ $\overline{20}$ $\overline{15}$ $\overline{18}$

$\overline{15}$ $\overline{14}$ $\overline{20}$ $\overline{8}$ $\overline{5}$ $\overline{21}$ $\overline{14}$ $\overline{4}$ $\overline{5}$ $\overline{18}$ $\overline{7}$ $\overline{18}$ $\overline{15}$ $\overline{21}$ $\overline{14}$ $\overline{4}$

$\overline{18}$ $\overline{1}$ $\overline{9}$ $\overline{12}$ $\overline{18}$ $\overline{15}$ $\overline{1}$ $\overline{4}$

Use the numbered alphabet to make a code to reveal another fact about Harriet Tubman.

GA1147

Frederick Augustus Douglass

Frederick Augustus Douglass was a great abolitionist and orator (one who speaks very well). Once when he spoke before the New York legislature on the subject of slavery, a legislator who heard him speak remarked that he would give anything to be able to speak like Frederick Douglass.

Douglass was born a slave in the state of Maryland in 1817. His mother was a slave, but his father was a white man. As a young boy Douglass was anxious to learn to read and write, but his master would not permit it. His master believed that if slaves were taught to read and write, they would want their freedom. Many slaves tried to learn secretly. Frederick was tutored secretly by his master's wife. When the master found that Frederick was learning to read, he became angry and beat him.

When Frederick was twenty-one years old, he escaped to New York. There he met and married a free black woman and they moved to Massachusetts. There he attended meetings held by the Massachusetts antislavery society. This was a group of people who wanted slaves to be free. At one of the society meetings, Frederick spoke on the subject of freedom. The society was so impressed with the way that he spoke that they hired him to travel and lecture to other people on slavery. For twenty-three years Frederick traveled in the northern United States, England, Scotland and Ireland. His travel was very difficult. He had to be careful. He was a runaway slave, and runaway slaves were treated harshly if they were caught. When Frederick spoke to people, he told of his hardship growing up as a slave, and he urged people to support the Anti-Slavery Movement so that slavery could be abolished.

During the Civil War, Frederick organized troops in Massachusetts. He was an advisor to President Lincoln and met with him on many occasions to discuss the problems of slavery. After the Civil War, Frederick served as U.S. marshall for Washington, D.C., and a recorder of deeds.

In 1847 Frederick bought his freedom and became a newspaper publisher. He published a paper called *North Star.* In it he continued to speak out against slavery. Frederick Douglass died in 1895, but he will always be remembered as the leading spokesman for black Americans in the 1800's.

GA1147

Douglass' Dozen

Fill the egg carton below with a dozen facts about Frederick Douglass. Put one fact in each egg cup.

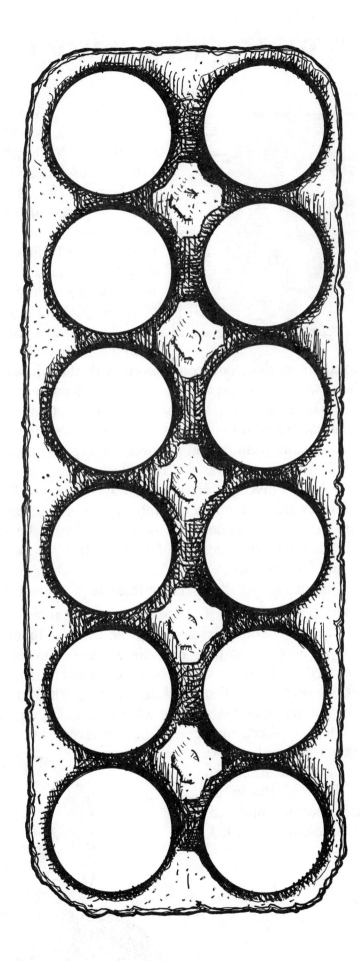

GA1147

Booker T. Washington and W.E.B. Du Bois

After the Civil War, two black leaders became famous. They were Booker Taliaferro Washington and William Edward Burghardt Du Bois. Washington was born in 1856; Du Bois was born in 1868. They were alike in many ways. They both came from poor families. They both received help from friends and neighbors to attend school. They were both well educated and both of them wanted to help black people have a better way of life. But they did not agree on how to help them. Washington believed that Blacks should learn a trade or vocation so that they could work with their hands to earn a living. He believed that Blacks would be respected more if they had money and owned property. In 1881 he founded Tuskegee Institute, a school that became famous for its agricultural research. It was on this campus that the famous Dr. George Washington Carver produced his many products of soybeans, peanuts and potatoes. Tuskegee is now a major university in Alabama. Booker T. Washington was the first black American to be elected to the Hall of Fame at New York University. He was an advisor to two Presidents, Theodore Roosevelt and William Howard Taft, on racial problems. In his best-selling autobiography, *Up from Slavery,* Booker T. Washington tells of his rise from slavery to become one of the most outstanding leaders and educators of his time. In 1940 the first postage stamp to honor a black person featured Booker T. Washington. Washington died on November 15, 1915. He is buried on the campus of Tuskeegee Institute in Alabama.

W.E.B. Du Bois disagreed with Booker T. Washington on what was best for Blacks. He felt that learning a trade or vocation was good, but he felt that Blacks should also have the opportunity to get a college education. He believed in the "talented tenth." That ten percent of the most talented black people should become trained leaders to fight for freedom and equality. In 1895 he became the first Black to receive a Ph.D. degree from Harvard University. Du Bois himself had many talents. He was an educator, an author, an historian, and a writer. In 1910 he helped organize one of the first civil rights groups in the United States. The organization was called the National Association for the Advancement of Colored People. He urged Blacks to register to vote and to become involved in politics. W.E.B. Du Bois died in 1963 at the age of 95.

GA1147

Washington/Du Bois Circles

Put the facts from the fact list in the circle named for each leader. Put the facts that tell of both leaders in the middle where the two circles meet.

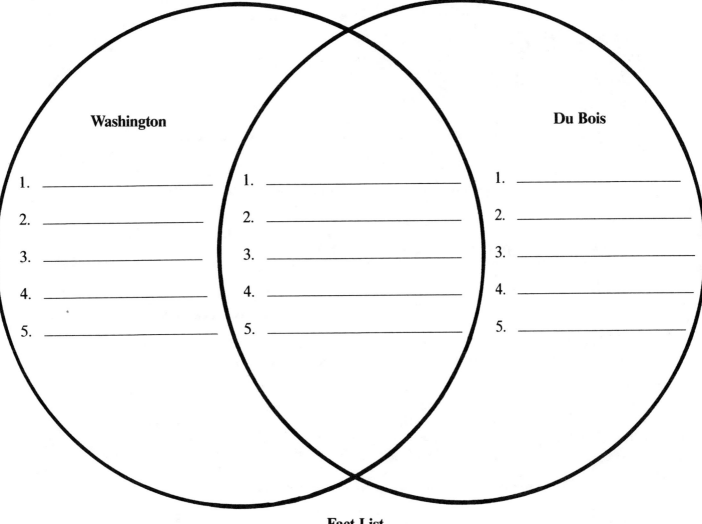

Washington

1. _____
2. _____
3. _____
4. _____
5. _____

1. _____
2. _____
3. _____
4. _____
5. _____

Du Bois

1. _____
2. _____
3. _____
4. _____
5. _____

Fact List

Received help from friends and neighbors to attend school

Born in 1868

Came from a poor family

Believed that Blacks should learn a vocation or trade

Wanted to help Blacks to have a better way of life

Organized the NAACP (National Association for the Advancement of Colored People)

Had a postage stamp issued in his honor

Was well-educated

Founded Tuskegee Institute

Died in 1963 at the age of 95

Was a great leader

Born in 1856

Elected to the Hall of Fame in New York

Believed in the "talented tenth"

Graduated from Harvard with a Ph.D. degree

23

GA1147

Escape!

Can you reach safety on the Underground Railroad? Write the correct answer in the blank at each "station."

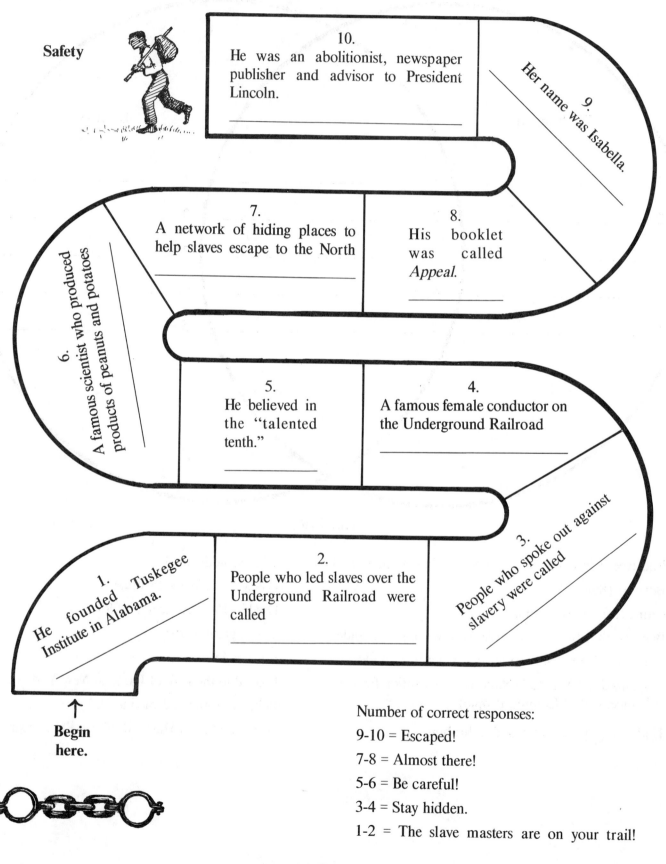

Safety

10. He was an abolitionist, newspaper publisher and advisor to President Lincoln.

_____

9. Her name was Isabella.

_____

7. A network of hiding places to help slaves escape to the North

_____

8. His booklet was called *Appeal.*

_____

6. A famous scientist who produced products of peanuts and potatoes

_____

5. He believed in the "talented tenth."

_____

4. A famous female conductor on the Underground Railroad

_____

3. People who spoke out against slavery were called

_____

1. He founded Tuskegee Institute in Alabama.

_____

2. People who led slaves over the Underground Railroad were called

_____

↑
Begin here.

Number of correct responses:

9-10 = Escaped!

7-8 = Almost there!

5-6 = Be careful!

3-4 = Stay hidden.

1-2 = The slave masters are on your trail!

GA1147

Dr. Martin Luther King, Jr.

Before 1954 black children could not attend the same school as white children. They could not sit and eat at the same lunch counter, they had to ride in the back of city buses and they had to drink from a water fountain with a sign that said "colored."

One day in December of 1955, a tired black woman named Rosa Parks got on a city bus in Montogomery, Alabama. There were no empty seats in the back of the bus so Mrs. Parks returned to the middle of the bus. She sat down. The bus driver came and told her to move to the back of the bus and stand up if she could not find an empty seat there. Mrs. Parks was tired. She refused to get up. The bus driver became angry. He had her arrested and sent to jail. Black people then became angry. They decided to do something about it.

A black minister named Martin Luther King, Jr., became their leader. He was the pastor of the Dexter Avenue Baptist Church in Montgomery. He held a meeting at his church, and Martin Luther King, Jr., and the people decided not to ride the city buses until segregation was ended. This was the beginning of the Montgomery bus boycott. Under Dr. King's leadership, 50,000 black people refused to ride the city buses. They walked to work for almost a year. Blacks were the main customers for the bus company. When they refused to ride the buses, the bus company lost money. Dr. King organized the Southern Christian Leadership Conference. He urged black people to use peaceful means to make people aware of the unfair treatment that Blacks were receiving. Dr. King traveled to many cities helping to organize sit-ins and demonstrations to gain equal rights for his people.

Finally, in 1956 the Supreme Court ruled that separate seats on a city bus for Whites and Blacks was unlawful. Dr. King and his people had used a nonviolent way to solve problems and make changes, and they had won.

Dr. King was jailed many times for his beliefs and actions in helping his people but he remained nonviolent. In August of 1963 Dr. King led over 200,000 people on a peace march on the nation's capital in Washington, D.C. It was on this occasion that he made his famous "I Have a Dream" speech. In 1964 he won the Nobel peace prize for his peaceful way of making changes. Dr. King was assassinated in Memphis, Tennessee, on April 4, 1968. Dr. King is buried in Atlanta, Georgia. On his grave are these words taken from his famous speech in Washington, D.C:

"Free at last, free at last,"
thank God Almighty, I'm free at last."

GA1147

The Noble Nobel

The Nobel peace prize is an international award given to the person who has made the greatest contributions toward promoting peace. Other Nobel prizes are given in the areas of physics, chemistry, physiology, medicine, literature and economics.

You have just been awarded a Nobel prize. Tell what area the prize was given for and why you deserve it.

Nobel prize for _____
(area)

Awarded to _____
(your name)

For _____
(Tell why you are receiving the prize.)

Role Play

Dr. Martin Luther King did not fight for freedom alone. Many people and events played a major role in his life. Tell the role that each of the following played in the life of Dr. King:

1. Rosa Parks _____

_____

2. The Southern Christian Leadership Conference _____

_____

3. The Nobel peace prize _____

_____

4. The Montgomery bus boycott_____

_____

5. Dexter Avenue Baptist Church _____

_____

GA1147

Jesse Jackson

Jesse Jackson was born in Greenville, South Carolina, on October 8, 1941. He grew up under the care of his mother and grandmother. When he was a young man, he participated in civil rights marches and demonstrations.

When Dr. Martin Luther King, Jr., was killed on April 4, 1968, black people became angry. Riots and violence broke out in many cities across America. Jesse Jackson spoke on television. He told black Americans to put down their rocks and bottles. He urged them to go back to the nonviolent way that Dr. King had taught them.

In 1970 two years after Dr. King's death, Jesse Jackson had become a well-known civil rights leader in the Southern Christian Leadership Conference. The SCLC had been organized by Dr. King to help black Americans use peaceful ways of gaining their equal rights.

At the age of twenty-seven, Jesse Jackson's picture appeared on the cover of *Time* magazine. He was one of the youngest Blacks ever to achieve this honor. By this time, Jackson had become an outstanding minister, a courageous leader, and a great spokesman. He served as a model for young people all over the United States.

In 1971 Jackson directed an organization called PUSH, People United to Save Humanity. As director, Jackson traveled to schools and churches throughout the United States speaking to young people of all colors and races. He talked to them about the importance of getting a good education. He talked to them about drugs and violence and about having a good attitude.

In November of 1983, Jackson announced that he would run for President of the United States. He knew that this would be a hard task. He would have to get enough votes to get his party's nomination—the Democratic party. Then he would have to run against the Republican candidate. But Jackson was willing to give it a try. His campaign slogan was "Run, Jesse Run." He traveled throughout the country talking to people. He talked about a "Rainbow Coalition." This meant bringing people of all races and colors together to work to make the United States a better place in which to live.

Jackson did not get his party's nomination for President, but he had inspired other black Americans to seek political and government offices, and he had started people thinking about the possibility of a black person becoming President of the United States.

On March 19, 1987, Jackson opened a campaign headquarters in Iowa and campaigned for the Democratic party's nomination. Again, he was unsuccessful, but this time he came close to being nominated by his party as the vice-presidential running mate for the presidential candidate. No one knows what the future holds for Jesse Jackson. As one of his supporters states, "Jackson is young and there are many more elections to come." If or when a black person is elected to be President of the United States, Jesse Jackson will be remembered as the one who started it all.

Today the Reverend Jesse Jackson is considered the best-known black person in the United States, and he is regarded as the most powerful black person in the world.

GA1147

Find It!

There are fifteen words about Jesse Jackson hidden in the puzzle below. Can you find them?

Here are the words to look for:

coalition	rainbow	humanity
democratic	run	organization
Greenville	violence	PUSH
minister	courageous	riots
people	great	time

```
D Q K U J A X U P Q C R S K R R M Q V W C O C V U
W B Y V B N C I M C I Q N N U E P Y J R N F E D F
R C L I W D I A D Y X B Z W T T I L S Y N Q E I W
A F N U L U T Y T I N A M U H S G G B A E M L I X
Y G W W C A A G B G F I O O B I W G I M O U J V E
K P C D N M R N K H F S S V F N L H C R A P V U A
W P F C Y U C E Q C I U O Y W I L B O Y I V A H P
K H L Z Y C O D F Y C H B B B K M N F F L V U M W X
J N N T J S M C H K M D S F T I H R L R K P F M F
A U W I Z S E L H G D K A M Y B B H P L S L E G T
B V B B T A D W M K S G T K K V W R X T V D Q U E
Y P E P P H C O W Z Y L P I K V O M O V E Q R K L
E Z O N B E L D C K O U T V P A M I W I L X J V L
H A A N V P J P O F S N Z H U X R O M G U E Z O I
E L P O E P R K U H N Z O R G A N I Z A T I O N V
E Z Z P W Y V Q R T C U F V V H M E A R R R Z Z N
Q V Q U R K X T A P F A R V V R R L R I A Q M O E
H E M D N W P A G K W O V Q F I V Q Z F I E L F E
I R J T E B T G E H A E A T X J O I T S N T Y P R
K N G N K C A O O W X V N R G W E L T P B T E X G
L D J Q C B Z I U C O A L I T I O N E M O A J E W
J L H K Q C E B S S K F M X T H N T Q N S W X N C H
H T A E R G T I M E F S R P U V E X E X C V C U A
B S V O R W D C B F X U W A F I T Z X K M E H H Y
T Y Y L U W F B J U M C S F J E Q I N B B S E A S
```

Use the fifteen words from the puzzle to complete the statements below.

1. At the age of 27, Jesse Jackson was pictured on the cover of _____ magazine.

2. Jesse directed an _____ called _____ .

3. Jesse wanted the nomination of the _____ party for President.

4. "_____, Jesse, Run" was Jesse's campaign slogan in 1983.

5. Jesse was an outstanding _____ .

6. "_____ _____" means bringing people of all races together.

7. Jesse was born in _____, South Carolina.

8. Jesse was a _____ leader and a _____ spokesman.

9. PUSH stands for _____ United to Save _____ .

10. When Dr. King was killed, _____ and _____ broke out in many cities in the United States.

28

GA1147

Honor Him

Is there a school or street in your community named for a famous black person? Many famous black Americans have been honored in this way. Others have been honored by receiving awards and prizes. Still others have had stamps and coins issued in their honor. Design a coin and stamp to honor Jesse Jackson.

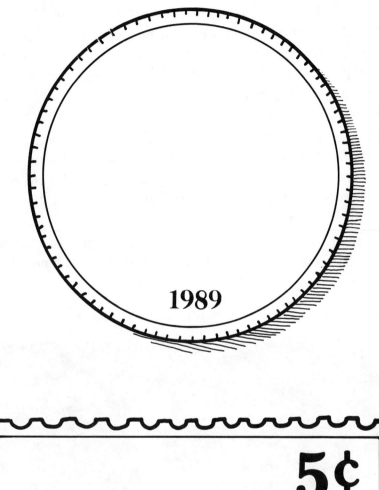

1989

5¢

GA1147

Black Inventors

Many inventions of the 1700's and 1800's were made by Blacks who worked as slaves. They invented tools and equipment to make their work easier. The federal government did not consider slaves to be United States citizens; therefore Blacks could not get a patent for their inventions. Henry Blair was the first black inventor to be granted a patent in the United States. He invented the corn planter in 1834. The patent meant that the idea was his very own and that he could manufacture and sell his planter.

After the Civil War during the industrial growth period in the South, many Blacks were granted patents for their inventions. Elijah McCoy alone had more than fifty patents for his inventions. In 1892 he invented a lubricating cup that fed oil to machinery without having to stop the machine. His invention became so popular that people today use the expression "the real McCoy" whenever they speak of something that is genuine or original.

Jan Matzeliger invented a machine to fasten the upper part of the shoe to the sole. Lewis Latimer made the drawings for Alexander Graham Bell's telephone and worked with Thomas Edison. Granville Woods held over thirty-five patents for his electrical inventions that he sold to American Bell Telephone and General Electric. He is sometimes called The Black Thomas Edison.

The list of black inventors continues to grow. In recent years Blacks have invented new kinds of elevators, refrigerators, golf tees, bathroom fixtures and electronic computer equipment.

GA1147

Footsteps of the Past

Listed below are ten inventors with their inventions and dates. Write the inventions in chronological order in the footstep patterns. Write the date below each answer.

Inventor	Invention	Date
1. Henry Blair	Corn planter	1834
2. Elijah McCoy	Lubrication for steam engine	1892
3. Garrett Morgan	Gas mask	1912
4. Garrett Morgan	Traffic light	1923
5. Jan Matzeliger	Shoe-lasting machine	1891
6. Lewis Latimer	Electric light bulb filament	1882
7. Granville T. Woods	Railway telegraph	1887
8. Benjamin Banneker	First clock	1761
9. George Grant	Golf tee	1899
10. Andrew Beard	A device to automatically join railroad cars when they bump	1897

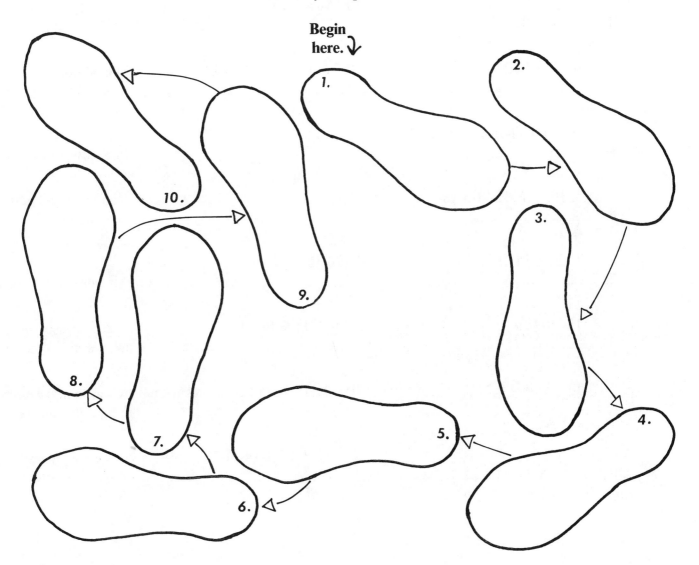

GA1147

Decoding

Directions:

Use the following code to fill in the blanks to find the names of ten modern black inventors.

A	B	C	D	E	F	G	H	I	J	K	L	M	N	O	P	Q	R	S	T	U	V	W	X	Y	Z
1	2	3	4	5	6	7	8	9	10	11	12	13	14	15	16	17	18	19	20	21	22	23	24	25	26

Name   **Invention**

1. 6-18-5-4-5-18-9-3-11   10-15-14-5-19   An X-ray machine
_____ _____

2. 13-1-18-22-9-14   19-20-5-23-1-18-4   An arithmetic unit for digital computers
_____ _____

3. 8-15-23-1-18-4   10-15-14-5-19   UHF antennae
_____ _____

4. 4-15-14-1-12-4   10-5-6-6-5-18-19-15-14   Digital storage system for computers
_____ _____

5. 20.-10.-13-1-18-19-8-1-12-12   Fire extinguisher
_____

6. 3.-10.-23-1-12-11-5-18   Cosmetics and hair care products
_____

7. 18-21-6-21-19   19-20-15-11-5-19   Air purification machine
_____ _____

8. 15-20-9-19   2-15-25-11-9-14-19   A device used in guided missiles and IBM computers
_____ _____

9. 13-5-18-5-4-9-20-8   7-15-21-18-4-9-14-5   A way to make electricity from a flowing gas
_____ _____

10. 22-1-14-3-5   13-1-18-3-8-2-1-14-11-19   A way to measure pilot fatigue in aircraft accidents
_____ _____

Easier and Safer

These black American inventors helped to make our lives safer and easier. In some factories, workers wear safety glasses to protect their eyes. Powell Johnson of Barton, Alabama, patented a design for eye protector glasses as early as 1880.

A clothes dryer saves time and work. George T. Sampson of Dayton, Ohio, invented a version of a clothes dryer in 1892.

A burning building! Firemen rushing up tall ladders, people climbing down! Joseph Winters of Chambersburg, Pennsylvania, invented a fire escape ladder for rescuing people from tall buildings in 1878. It could rescue people quickly and safely because it was attached to the fire truck.

Do you have a bicycle? Does it have a basket for carrying books or baseball gloves? In 1899 Jerry Certain of Tampa, Florida, patented a basket carrier for the bicycle.

A bridle bit is used to control the horse and make it respond to the rider's command. Lincoln Brown of Xenia, Ohio, patented a bridle bit in 1892.

Have you ever walked to the street corner to mail a letter? Did you put it in a big blue mailbox? Phillip Downing of Boston, Massachusetts, designed and patented the big, blue mailbox in 1891.

A device to keep elevators from moving while passengers get on or off was patented by Alexander Miles of Duluth, Minnesota.

When bakers make large amounts of dough for doughnuts, cakes, biscuits and pies, the dough is heavy and hard to mix by hand. Joseph Lee of Auburndale, Massachusetts, helped to solve this problem. He patented a kneading machine in 1894.

Have you ever mopped the kitchen floor? Thomas Stewart of Detroit, Michigan, patented his mop design in 1893.

In earlier days, if your teacher asked you to write your book report in ink, you would have to carry a separate bottle of ink to dip your pen in before writing. In 1890 William Purvis of Philadelphia, Pennsylvania, invented a fountain pen that carried its own ink.

If you cut your grass with a lawn mower, you can thank John Albert Burr of Agawam, Massachusetts, for making this chore safer. He patented a device in 1899 that helped to keep grass from clogging the gears.

GA1147

Greetings

Write the correct name in each blank on these thank-you letters.

Dear Mr. _____,

Thank you for inventing the bridle bit. It helps me to control my horse, and it makes him so much fun to ride.

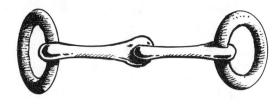

Dear Mr. _____,

Thank you for inventing the bicycle carrier. Now I can throw my baseball glove in the basket and hold on with both hands when the neighbor's dog chases me.

Dear Mr. _____,

My father is a fireman. Thank you for helping to make his job easier and safer with your invention of the fire escape ladder.

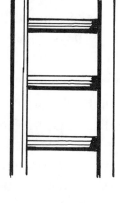

Dear Mr. _____,

My Uncle Jim works in a pie pan factory. He wears safety glasses to protect his eyes. Thank you for inventing safety glasses. My uncle Jim is such a nice man.

Dear Mr. _____,

My grandmother is a little slow in getting off elevators. Thank you for inventing a device to make elevators stop so that people can get off and on.

ELEVATOR

GA1147

Thank You

Now write your own thank-you letters from the greetings that are given.

Dear Mr. Burr,

_____

_____

_____

Dear Mr. Downing,

_____

_____

_____

Dear Mr. Lee,

_____

_____

_____

Dear Mr. Purvis,

_____

_____

_____

Dear Mr. Sampson,

_____

_____

_____

GA1147

Garrett Morgan
1877-1963

On July 25, 1916, an explosion at the Cleveland Waterworks ripped through a tunnel, trapping underground workers. Deadly gases and heavy smoke filled the underground spaces making it difficult to rescue the workers. Finally, someone in the crowd remembered a black man who had won a grand prize at the Second International Exposition of Sanitation and Safety. His invention was a gas mask and his name was Garrett Morgan. Morgan had received a patent for his gas mask and had begun to sell it, but when it was discovered that he was black, many orders were cancelled. However, Morgan continued to perfect his mask. On the day of the explosion, he was asked to bring his gas mask to the area. He used his gas mask and led a team of rescue workers into the tunnel where workers were trapped beneath the ground. Thirty-two men were led to safety. His masks were later used to protect World War I soldiers from deadly gas fumes. In 1923 Morgan invented yet another useful device. He invented an automatic stop sign, the ancestor of today's traffic light.

It is hard to estimate how many lives were saved by Morgan's inventions. He received many awards and citations for his inventions. At the Emancipation Centennial Celebration in Chicago in August of 1963, Morgan was nationally recognized. Morgan did not attend. He had died one month earlier.

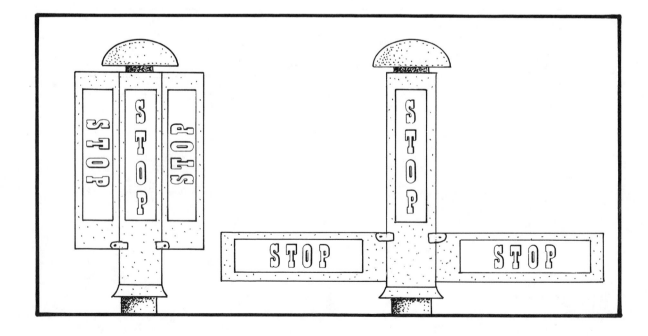

36

Safety Scientist

Garrett Morgan has been called the Safety Scientist. Write a paragraph telling why you think he deserves this title.

_____

_____

_____

_____

_____

Draw a picture of Garrett Morgan using his gas mask to rescue trapped underground workers.

GA1147

Inventor's Award

The time is in the future. You have become a great inventor. Complete the award certificate below about your invention.

The International Awards Committee Has Awarded the First Grand Trophy Prize to

_____

(your name)

For His/Her Invention of

_____

Draw a picture of your invention in this space. Also tell how it works.

38

Black Writers

Black writers had their beginning during slavery.

Maya Angelou was born in St. Louis, Missouri. She has written, produced and appeared in many shows for National Education Television. Her famous book, *I Know Why the Caged Bird Sings*, was published in 1970.

James Baldwin was born in Harlem, New York. His novel *Go Tell It on the Mountain* was published in 1953. *The Fire Next Time* and *Nobody Knows My Name* are two of his most famous books.

Arna Bontemps was born in Alexandria, Louisiana. His first novel, *God Sends Sunday*, was published in 1931. Bontemps has written children's books, biographies, poetry and a Broadway play.

Gwendolyn Brooks was born in Topeka, Kansas. In 1950 she became the first Black to be awarded a Pulitzer prize. She was awarded the prize for her volume of poems *Annie Allen*.

Paul Laurence Dunbar was born in Dayton, Ohio. He began writing poems at the age of six. At age thirteen, he gave a public recital of his poetry. One of his books of poems *Lyrics of Lowly Life* won him national recognition in 1896.

Nikki Giovanni, born in Knoxville, Tennessee, is the author of several books of poetry. Her volume *Black Feelings, Black Talk* was published in 1968.

Alex Haley was born in Ithaca, New York. He wrote his award-winning book *Roots: The Saga of an American Family* in 1976.

Lorraine Hansberry was born in Chicago, Illinois. In 1959 her play *A Raisin in the Sun* opened on Broadway. It was the first play written by a black woman to be produced on Broadway. It was also the first black play to win the Best Play of the Year Award from the New York Drama Critics Circle.

Jupiter Harmon, a slave of Queens Village, Long Island, was the first black poet in America. His book of poems was published in 1761.

Langston Hughes was born in Joplin, Missouri. He wrote his first volume of poetry in 1926, *The Weary Blues*. During his lifetime he published ten volumes of poetry and sixty-six short stories. In 1956 he wrote an autobiography, *I Wonder as I Wander*.

Mildred Taylor was born in Jackson, Mississippi, and grew up in Toledo, Ohio. In 1976 her book *Roll of Thunder, Hear My Cry* was published. In 1977 it won the Newberry medal.

Douglas Turner Ward was born in Burnside, Louisiana. His play *Day of Absence* ran for more than a year at the St. Marks Playhouse in New York City (1965-66).

Phillis Wheatley was born in Africa. She was sold as a slave when she was eight years old. When she became ill in 1773, she was sent to England to recover. It was there that her volume *Poems on Various Subjects, Religious and Moral* was published.

GA1147

Bookshelf

Write the correct author's name on each book in the library. Select names from the name bank below. Write the date of publication on the line beneath the book.

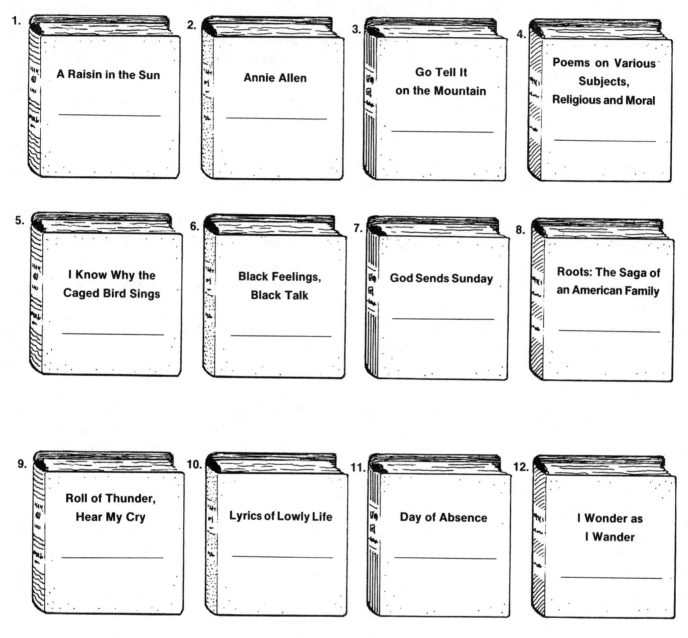

1. A Raisin in the Sun _____

2. Annie Allen _____

3. Go Tell It on the Mountain _____

4. Poems on Various Subjects, Religious and Moral _____

5. I Know Why the Caged Bird Sings _____

6. Black Feelings, Black Talk _____

7. God Sends Sunday _____

8. Roots: The Saga of an American Family _____

9. Roll of Thunder, Hear My Cry _____

10. Lyrics of Lowly Life _____

11. Day of Absence _____

12. I Wonder as I Wander _____

Name Bank

Maya Angelou
Lorraine Hansberry
Alex Haley
Phillis Wheatley
Gwendolyn Brooks
Nikki Giovanni

James Baldwin
Langston Hughes
Paul Laurence Dunbar
Arna Bontemps
Douglas Ward Turner
Mildred Taylor

GA1147

Contemporary Black Writers

Imamu Amiri Baraka (LeRoi Jones) was born in Newark, New Jersey, in 1934. He writes plays, novels, short stories and poems.

Victor Hernandez Cruz is a native of Puerto Rico. His first collection of poetry was published in 1968.

James Emanuel was born in 1921. He received his Ph.D. from Columbia University in 1962. He teaches English at City University of New York. His book *Langston Hughes* was published in 1967.

Marie Evans is a native of Toledo, Ohio. Her poetry appears in American and European magazines and in textbooks.

Julia Fields was born in Uniontown, Alabama. Her book *Poems* was published in 1968.

Nikki Giovanni was born in Knoxville, Tennessee. She writes poems, short stories and essays.

Bobb Hamilton is a poet and short story writer. He lives in New York City. He teaches black literature and history at Queens College and edits *Soulbook*, a popular magazine.

Mae Jackson is a native of Arkansas who now lives in New York. She is a song writer and a singer.

Norman Jordan is a native West Virginian. He is a playwright and a poet. He now lives in Cleveland, Ohio.

William Alfred MacLean, Jr., wrote a poem called "War" that was published in 1969 when he was only ten years old. He is a native of New York City.

Clarence Major was born in Atlanta, Georgia. He writes novels, magazine articles and poetry.

Quandra Prettyman was born in Baltimore, Maryland. She is a college teacher and book editor in New York City.

Sonia Sanchez is a native of Birmingham, Alabama. Her poems are published in many American magazines.

Larry Thompson was born in 1950 in Seneca, South Carolina. While attending Yale University he was editor of the *Yale Literary Magazine*. He is also a poet.

Margaret Walker is a native of Birmingham. She wrote a prize-winning novel called *Jubilee*. It was published in 1966.

GA1147

Annual Great Writers' Awards

You are the emcee for the annual great writers' awards ceremony. Place the name of each writer on the correct certificate list so that you will not get them mixed up on awards night.

Books and Novels

_____

_____

_____

_____

Short Stories

_____

_____

_____

_____

Songs and Plays

_____

_____

_____

_____

Poetry

_____

_____

_____

_____

_____

_____

_____

_____

_____

_____

_____

_____

Editors

_____

_____

_____

Write one of your own prize-winning poems below.

GA1147

Alex Haley

Alex Haley was born in Ithaca, New York, in 1921. He grew up in the small town of Henning, Tennessee. On warm summer evenings his grandmother and her sisters (his great aunts) would sit on the front porch and talk of "old times." Alex graduated from high school at the age of 15 and joined the Coast Guard. It was there that he began his writing career. Writing helped to pass the time away on long voyages at sea. In 1959 he retired from the Coast Guard to become a full-time writer. He remembered the warm summer evenings on the front porch and the conversations of his aunts and grandmother. Alex spent twelve years collecting information about his family and ancestors. During this time he searched old family records at fifty different libraries and traveled to three different continents. He traced his family back two hundred years.

In 1976 he completed his research work. He wrote a book of his findings. It was called *Roots: The Saga of an American Family*. It was the biggest, best-selling book in the United States. In 1977 *Roots* was made into a television mini-series movie. It was watched by more people than any other program in the history of television. For *Roots*, Haley won the Pulitzer prize and the National Book Award, two of the most outstanding awards in the field of literature.

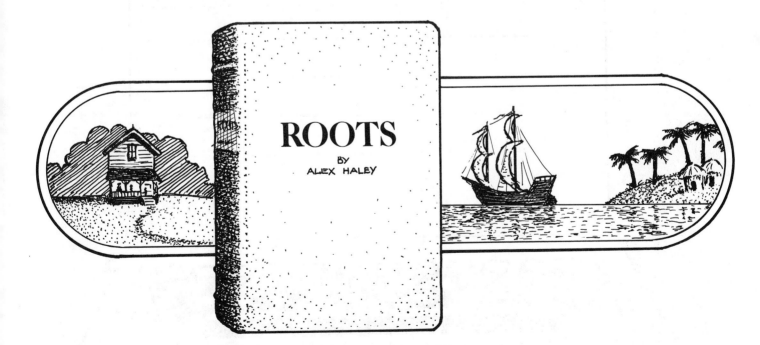

ROOTS
BY
ALEX HALEY

GA1147

Author! Author!

Complete the story.

It was a warm summer day; I dozed beneath the big oak tree in my own backyard. Suddenly I heard a loud noise. It was coming from the window of my house.

44

Discover Your Roots

Directions:

Complete the family tree to discover your roots. Ask your parents for help if you need it.

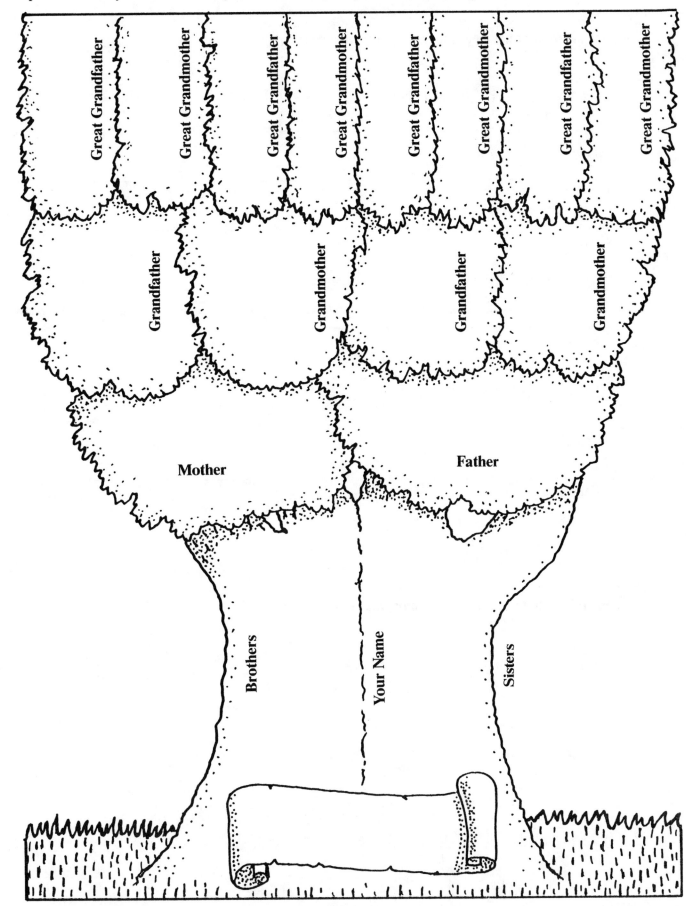

GA1147

This Is Us!

Directions:

Complete the information below for each family member.

Name	Favorite Food	Favorite TV Show	Hobby
_____ (You)	_____	_____	_____
_____ (Mother)	_____	_____	_____
_____ (Father)	_____	_____	_____
_____ (Brother)	_____	_____	_____
_____ (Sister)	_____	_____	_____
_____ (Other)	_____	_____	_____
_____ (Other)	_____	_____	_____
_____ (Other)	_____	_____	_____

List some things that you have in common with other family members.

Black Artists

Sculptors

When you think of an artist, do you think only of a person who paints or draws a picture? Art can take many forms. Some artists are called sculptors. They take material such as clay or metal and mold it into a figure or design. One such artist was a black woman named Edmonia Lewis. She lived from 1845 to 1890. She was the first American black woman to be recognized for sculptor work. She made bust figures of such famous people as Abraham Lincoln and Henry Wadsworth Longfellow, an outstanding American poet. The Longfellow bust was made for the Harvard College Library. Her first work was exhibited in Chicago in 1870 and in Rome, Italy, in 1871. Her interest in art began to grow when she attended Oberlin College in 1865. It was there that her artwork was noticed by a famous sculptor, Edmund Brackett of Boston, Massachusetts. He helped her to start a career as a sculptor. Edmonia spent most of her adult life in Italy, but she returned to America during her later years where she lived until her death around 1890.

Geraldine McCullough was a black woman sculptor and painter. She was born in Maywood, a Chicago suburb, on December 1, 1922. She used metal to construct beautiful objects. In 1964 her sculpture called *Phoenix* received the George Widener Memorial Gold Medal at the Pennsylvania Academy of Fine Arts. This was unusual because Geraldine had not been invited to enter her art in the contest. Only well-known artists had been invited to show their work. Geraldine McCullough not only entered her work without an invitation but she won. She appeared on television programs, and magazine reporters wrote about her in national magazines such as *Time* and *Ebony*. In 1966 she received an invitation from the Soviet government to visit Moscow and Leningrad as a guest artist.

Richard Hunt has been called the Master of Metals. He works with a blowtorch, a hammer and sheets of metal to create art. Some of his structures are twelve feet high, two feet taller than a basketball goal. Hunt's work has been shown at museums in New York City, Chicago, Senegal and the National Museum in Tel Aviv, Israel. Hunt is a native of Chicago, Illinois. He was born in 1935.

Marion Perkins is another famous black sculptor. He was born in 1908 and died in 1961. He first began to sculpt from bars of soap as he worked selling papers at a newsstand on Chicago's Southside. His work was noticed by Si Gordon who taught him to model in clay, plaster, mold and cast, and stone. In 1951 his sculpture *Man of Sorrow* won the Art Institute of Chicago sculpture prize.

Richard Barthé is called a modern sculptor. He was born in Mississippi in 1901. In 1924 he entered the Art Institute of Chicago and began painting until one of his teachers encouraged him to work at sculpture. He did and within two years he presented a one-man art show of his work. His first work was a bust of Toussaint L'Ouverture, a French slave who led a revolt in the Republic of Haiti. His work is exhibited in museums in New York City, Ohio, Pennsylvania, Atlanta and other cities in the United States. His work can also be seen in collections in England, Germany, France, Africa, Canada, the Virgin Islands and Haiti.

GA1147

Whose Hands?

Directions:

Match the hand of the sculptor on the left with his work on the right.

Edmonia Lewis

Marion Perkins

Richard Hunt

Richard Barthé

Geraldine McCullough

_____ 1. *Man of Sorrow*

_____ 2. Twelve feet high metal structures

_____ 3. Bust of Abraham Lincoln

_____ 4. Bust of Toussaint L'Ouverture

_____ 5. *Phoenix*

Mystery Sculptor

Dial these numbers to find the name of the mystery sculptor.

7424273-4868

_____

GA1147

Muralists, Painters and Cartoonist

Charles H. Alston is a black muralist. A muralist is an artist who paints pictures on walls. His mural designs can be seen in the Hall of Forestry and in the Hall of Invertebrate Biology at the Museum of National History in Washington, D.C. Alston is also an illustrator. He has drawn pictures for *Fortune, Redbook, Collier's, The New Yorker* and *Mademoiselle* magazines. Alston was born in Charlotte, North Carolina, in 1907, but moved to New York as a boy. In 1968 he became a teacher at City College of New York. His most recent mural was called *Man on the Threshold of Space.* It can be seen at the Harriet Tubman School in Manhattan, New York. A picture of Charles Alston's painting *Family* was featured in the February, 1989 issue of *Instructor* magazine.

William Harper and Aaron Douglas were two other black muralists. The mural paintings of Harper can be seen in public buildings in Illinois, Indiana and New York. Douglas' mural paintings are displayed at Fisk University, Nashville, Tennessee, and Bennett College in Greensboro, North Carolina.

Robert Duncanson was a famous black artist of the 1840's and 50's. He was born in 1821. He painted murals, landscapes and portraits. He began to do sketches when he was a teenager. In 1840 the Freedmen's Aid Society of Ohio collected enough money to send him to school in Glasgow, Scotland. His works have been displayed in the United States as well as England and Scotland. One of his famous paintings is called *Blue Hole.* It is displayed in the Cincinnati Art Museum in Ohio.

Edward M. Bannister was a landscape painter. He lived from 1828 to 1901. During his lifetime he was known as one of America's best landscape artists. Once he entered a painting in the Centennial Exhibition in Philadelphia. He called his painting *Under the Oaks.* His painting took the Gold Medal. When the judges found that Bannister was black, they wanted to withdraw the medal from him, but others insisted that the judges' decision remained. So, Bannister kept his prize. Later that year he sold *Under the Oaks* for $15.00. That was quite a bit of money in 1876!

One day a thirteen-year-old boy watched a painter at work. To him it was like magic the way the painter turned colors and drawings into interesting pictures. The boy decided then and there that he wanted to be a painter. He had no idea of the studying and learning that it takes to be a good painter, but he studied hard and within a few years he had become one of the greatest artists of his time. The boy who grew up to be a famous artist was Henry O. Tanner. In 1896 one of his famous paintings *The Resurrection of Lazarus* was hailed by the artistic world as a masterpiece. The *Lazarus* painting was purchased by the French Government. After this, Tanner received many awards and prizes for his work.

GA1147

Melvin Gray Johnson lived from 1896 to 1934. He died at the age of 38. Melvin was born and grew up in poverty in Greensboro, North Carolina, but with the help of others, he managed to study at the New York Academy of Designs. Melvin Johnson was known for his paintings of the life of black people in the South. His best paintings of this type were *Dixie Madonna, Ruby, Brothers, Red Road* and *Convict Labor.*

Charles White grew up as a poor boy in the slums of Chicago in 1918. His first paintings were done on the window shades of his home; then he began painting on buildings. When he was fifteen, he displayed his artwork in empty stores, churches, vacant lots, anywhere that he thought people would stop and notice his work. He was finally able to study at the Art Institute of Chicago. His art was named for many of the black spiritual songs that are sung in some black churches. His art may be seen in art museums throughout the United States and abroad. *Move on Up a Little Higher* and *Mary Don't You Weep* are among the best in his art collection.

Do you enjoy reading cartoons in the newspaper or magazines? Do you like to draw cartoons? If so, maybe you can draw some for your school newspaper or maybe you can draw some and display them at home or in your classroom. E. Simms Campbell was a famous black cartoonist. He began drawing cartoons for his high school newspaper in St. Louis. After his graduation he studied at the Chicago Art Institute. When he first tried to sell his cartoons, he was told that it was a waste of time for a young black boy to try to make a living drawing cartoons. However, Campbell continued to draw. Finally *Esquire* magazine spotted some of his cartoons. His cartoon called "Cuties" appeared in more than 100 different newspapers in the United States. His cartoons have also appeared in *The New Yorker, Cosmopolitan* and *Ebony* magazines. Campbell died in 1971.

Complete It!

Directions:

Complete the statements with names from the word bank.

1. Two artists who worked for *The New Yorker* and *Cosmopolitan* magazines were:

   _____ and _____

2. _____ painted the religious picture *The Resurrection of Lazarus.*

3. _____ painted *Mary Don't You Weep.*

4. _____ was a black cartoonist.

5. _____ painted murals for public buildings in Illinois, Indiana and New York.

6. _____ painted the life of black people in the South.

7. _____ America's best landscape artist.

8. _____ painted *Man on the Threshold of Space.*

9. _____ painted murals for Fisk University in Nashville.

10. _____ *Blue Hole* was one of his famous paintings.

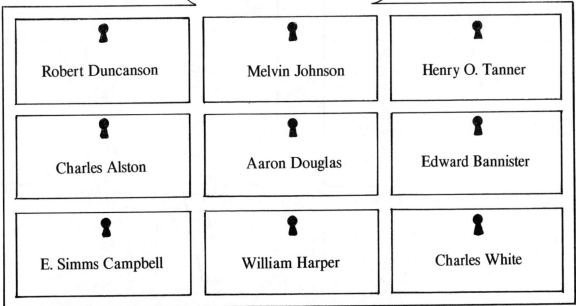

WORD BANK

Robert Duncanson	Melvin Johnson	Henry O. Tanner
Charles Alston	Aaron Douglas	Edward Bannister
E. Simms Campbell	William Harper	Charles White

GA1147

My Art Gallery

Congratulations! You have been asked by the Academy of Fine Arts of your city to do a One-Man Art Show. Use pencils, felt tip pens, or crayons to show the four pictures that you will display at the Academy of Fine Arts Show.

52

GA1147

Black Doctors

Black doctors have been active in the field of medicine since early Colonial days. One of the first black men of medicine was Dr. Lucas Santomée of New York. He trained in Holland and practiced medicine during both the Dutch and English control of New York. In 1667 he was given a plot of land for his services to the colony of New Amsterdam.

In 1791 Oneissimus, an African slave, developed an *antidote* for smallpox. During the 1780's, James Derham became one of the most *prominent* physicians in New Orleans. In 1837 James McCune Smith of New York became the first black doctor to earn a medical degree. He attended school in Glasgow, Scotland, and earned his degree there. In 1876 two major medical schools for Blacks were established in the United States— Howard University School of Medicine at Washington, D.C., and Meharry Medical School in Nashville, Tennessee. This made it possible for thousands of black students to study and practice medicine. The first hospital for black patients was established in Savannah, Georgia, in 1833. It was called the Georgia Infirmary.

In 1891 Provident Hospital of Chicago was founded. It was here that Dr. Daniel Hale Williams performed the first open heart surgery in history.

Dr. Theodore Lawless in Chicago was one of the world's leading *dermatologists.* People from all walks of life jammed his office for treatment of skin ailments. In 1929 Dr. Lawless won the Harmon Award for Outstanding Achievement in Medicine. He attended Talledega College in Alabama and earned his medical degree from Northwestern University in Evanston, Illinois. He taught medicine at this university for more than fifteen years. Dr. Lawless has been honored many times for his outstanding work in medicine. He died in 1971.

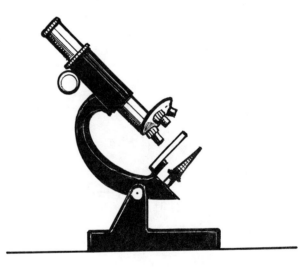

Dr. Ulysses Grant Dailey was one of the most distinguished surgeons in America. After graduating from Northwestern University Medical School, he spent four years as an assistant to Dr. Daniel Hale Williams, the outstanding doctor and founder of Provident Hospital in Chicago. In 1926 Dr. Dailey set up his own hospital. His brilliant mind and steady fingers made him an *exceptional* surgeon of great fame throughout the world. Dr. Daily died in 1971.

Three black women were among the first black doctors to earn M.D. degrees in the United States. Dr. Rebecca Lee received a medical degree from the New England Female Medical College in 1864. Dr. Rebecca Cole received a degree in medicine from the Woman's Medical College in Philadelphia in 1867. Dr. Susan Smith-Steward received her medical degree from New York Medical College and Hospital for Women in 1870.

Today, many great black doctors continue to make outstanding contributions in the field of medicine.

 GA1147

Medical Time Tunnel

Arrange the events below in the time tunnel in chronological order.

Provident Hospital in Chicago was founded.

The first hospital for black patients was established.

Two major medical schools for Blacks were established.

James McCune Smith became the first black doctor to earn a medical degree in the United States.

Dr. Ulysses Grant Dailey, an exceptional surgeon, set up his own hospital.

Dr. Theodore Lawless won the Harmon Award for Outstanding Achievement in Medicine.

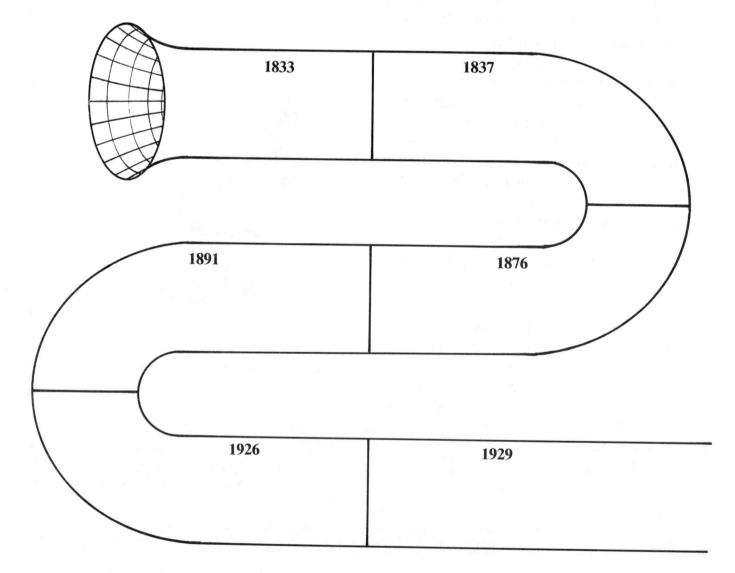

GA1147

Black Scientists

In 1985 the CIBA-GEIGY Corporation selected fifteen scientists and doctors for their Exceptional Black Scientist Poster Series. These scientists and doctors were selected for their outstanding contributions in the field of science and medicine.

Dr. Percy Julian, a famous research chemist, developed an inexpensive method of making cortisone, a drug used to treat arthritis. He also developed a synthetic drug used to treat an eye disease called glaucoma.

Dr. Jewel Cobb, Dr. LaSalle D. Leffall, Jr., and **Dr. Jane Wright** are outstanding in the field of cancer research.

Dr. Ernest Just was considered to be one of the world's most distinguished scientists in the field of biology. His most important work was done with the study of the cell and fertilization. He was the author of two books and sixty scientific papers. During his college years at Dartmouth College of New Hampshire, he excelled and graduated magna cum laude (with high honor) and Phi Beta Kappa.

Dr. David Blackwell, an outstanding mathematician, has served as professor of math at the University of California (Berkeley) since 1954.

Dr. Lloyd Ferguson, a chemist, is the author of six college chemistry textbooks.

Dr. Reatha Clark King is a pioneer in chemical research. She is also president of Metropolitan State University, St. Paul, Minnesota.

Dr. Samuel Kountz was an international leader in transplant surgery. He performed more than five hundred kidney transplants during his lifetime.

Dr. Augustus White, III helped improve treatment for spinal injuries.

Dr. Shirley Jackson, physicist, was the first American black woman to earn a doctorate degree from (MIT) Massachusetts Institute of Technology.

Dr. Walter E. Massey, physicist and educator, became professor of physics and dean of the college at Brown University at age 36.

Dr. Jennie R. Patrick was the first black woman in the United States to earn a doctorate in chemical engineering.

Dr. Charles R. Drew's research in blood preservation led to the founding of blood banks.

Dr. W. Montague Cobb, anatomist and medical instructor, served as faculty member at Howard University Medical School for fifty-one years.

In the laboratory, in the doctor's office and in the hospitals across America, black scientists and doctors are at work helping to prevent and treat diseases and to make our lives better each day.

GA1147

Official Scientists

Directions:

Use the names in the name bank to put each scientist in his/her correct office.

Name Bank

Jewel Cobb	Jane Wright	David Blackwell	Samuel Kountz
Shirley Jackson	Ernest Just	Lloyd Ferguson,	Reatha Clark King
Walter Massey	Percy Julian	Charles Drew	W. Montague Cobb

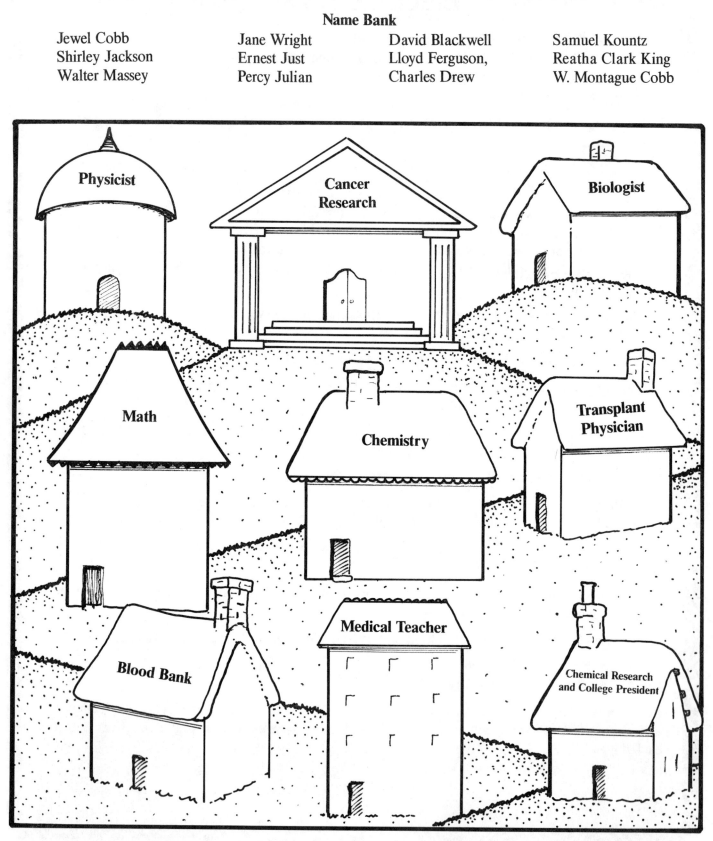

Choose one of these scientists of special interest to you. Research his/her life and accomplishments and share your findings with other members of your class.

GA1147

Guion S. Bluford, Jr.

Guion Stewart Bluford, Jr., was born on November 22, 1942 in Philadelphia, Pennsylvania. His mother was a special education teacher and his father was a mechanical engineer. When he was young, Guion (pronounced Guy-on) liked to play with model airplanes. He liked to build them and take them apart. He wanted to be an aerospace engineer—a person who designs, builds and flies a spacecraft. Guion attended Overbrook High School. Because he was not a straight "A" student, his guidance counselor said that he should not go to college. He was told that a technical school would be best for him, but Guion was determined to go to college to study to be an aerospace engineer. Guion enrolled at Penn State University and graduated in 1964 with a Bachelor of Science degree. Guion then married, moved to Arizona and trained as a pilot at Williams Air Force Base. While attending Penn State, he had enrolled in ROTC (Reserve Officers Training Corps) and received the ROTC Distinguished Military Graduate award.

In 1965 he received his wings and became a pilot flying combat missions over Vietnam. Guion then enrolled in the Air Force Institute of Technology. He graduated from the Institute in 1972 with a Master's degree in aerospace engineering. Finally, Guion was beginning to see his dream fulfilled. He went to work at the Air Force Flight Dynamic Laboratory in Ohio. There he tested and designed aircrafts. Guion continued his education. In 1978 when he was only 35 years old, Guion received his Ph.D. in aerospace engineering. That same year he applied for NASA Astronaut Training Program. Guion and 8878 people applied for the training program. Guion was selected and began training at the Space Flight Center in Houston, Texas. Guion's excitement of space travel began to grow. He completed training and was selected to fly aboard the spaceship *Challenger* on its third flight. The time finally came. All of Guion's waiting, training and education would pay off. On August 30, 1983, he was one of five crew members who blasted off into space aboard the spaceship *Challenger*. The mission was successful and *Challenger* returned to earth on September 5, 1983. Lieutenant Colonel Guion Stewart Bluford, Jr., had earned a place in history. He became the first black American to fly in space. His dream of becoming an aerospace engineer was completely fulfilled.

57

GA1147

Challenger Time Line

Write the important events in the life of Guion Bluford beneath each date in the space shuttle *Challenger*.

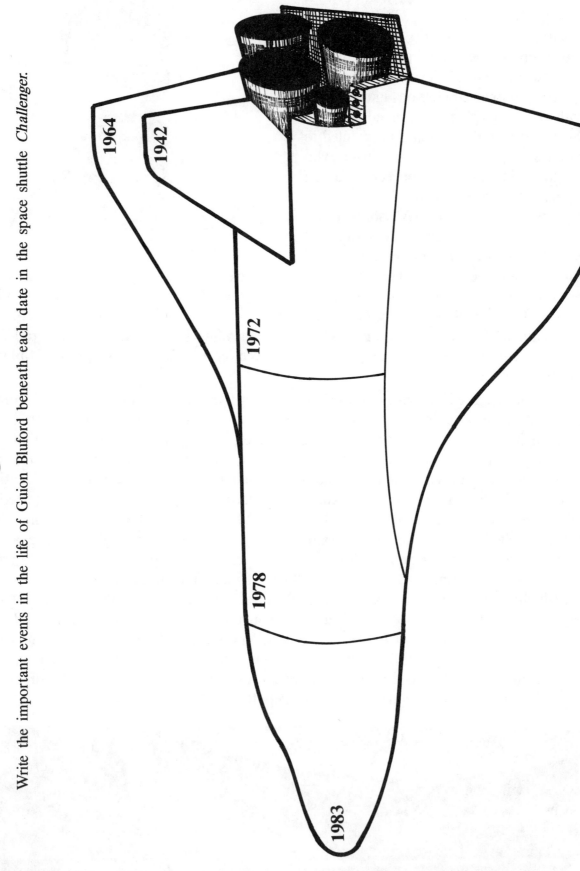

1964

1942

1965

1972

1978

1983

Aerospace Engineer

An aerospace engineer designs, builds and flies a spacecraft. Imagine that you are an aerospace engineer. Design one of the following spacecrafts:

A. A Space Cruiser

B. A Space Fighter

C. A Space Explorer

D. A Space Station

E. A Space Shuttle

Blacks in Government

During the reconstruction years following the Civil War, Congress wrote amendments to the Constitution and passed several laws. These laws were passed to protect the rights of black people. One of these laws gave Blacks the right to vote. This made it possible for Blacks to be elected to positions in state and federal government. Between 1869 and 1901 twenty-two Blacks from the South were elected to the United States Congress.

John Willis Menard of Louisiana was the first Black elected to Congress, but he never served because the election was challenged. In 1869 the state of Georgia sent Jefferson Long to Congress. He was the first Black to actually serve in Congress. Alabama sent three representatives to Congress. They were Jeremiah Haralson, James Rapier and Benjamin Turner. James O'Hara, Henry Cheatham and John Hyman represented North Carolina. South Carolina elected eight representatives: Richard Cain, Robert Elliott, George Murray, Robert Delarge, Thomas Miller and Alonzo Ransier. Joseph Rainey and Robert Smalls served five terms each in the U.S. Congress. Hiram Revels and Blanche Bruce served as senators from Mississippi. Revels served from 1870 to 1871. He was elected to fill the term of Jefferson Davis, the former president of the Confederacy. Bruce served from 1875 to 1881. John R. Lynch represented Mississippi in the U.S. Congress and Josiah Walls represented Florida.

John Mercer Langston represented Virginia in the U.S. Congress. Charles Nash was a representative of Louisiana—the only representative from Louisiana that was elected and seated in Congress.

In 1871 Pickney Benton Stewart Pinchback served as lieutenant and acting governor of Louisiana. Oscar Dunn and C.C. Antoine also served as lieutenant governor of that state. Two Blacks served as lieutenant governor of the state of South Carolina. They were Alonzo Ransier in 1870 and Richard Graves in 1874. Jonathan Wright was an associate justice of the South Carolina State Supreme Court and Francis Cardoza served as secretary of state and state treasurer.

In 1872 Samuel Lee was speaker of the house of the South Carolina House of Representatives. A.K. Davis served as lieutenant governor of the state of Mississippi in 1873.

Between 1868-1872 Johnathan Gibbs served as secretary of state and state superintendent of schools in the state of Florida.

Oscar De Priest was the first congressman of the 20th century. De Priest was born in Florence, Alabama, on March 9, 1871, and later moved to Chicago. In 1928 he was elected as a Republican to the U.S. House of Representatives.

GA1147

Let's Take a Poll

Directions:

Make a state poll to show the number of Blacks elected to Congress during reconstruction.

Alabama _____ Georgia _____ North Carolina _____

South Carolina _____ Louisiana _____ Mississippi _____

Florida _____ Virginia _____

Complete the bar graph to show the representation of Blacks in Congress.

	1	2	3	4	5	6	7	8
Alabama	▓	▓	▓					
Florida								
Georgia								
Louisiana								
Mississippi								
North Carolina								
South Carolina								
Virginia								

Pioneer Politicians

Thurgood Marshall—Baltimore, Maryland, first black associate justice of the Supreme Court (1967)

Shirley Chisholm—Brooklyn, New York, first black congresswoman (1968)

Constance Motley—New Haven, Connecticut, first black woman judge in New York Federal District Court

Jesse Jackson—Greenville, South Carolina, first Black to campaign for President for two consecutive terms (1984 and 1988)

Arthur Mitchell—Chambers County, Alabama, first Black to address a national Democratic Convention (1934)

John Conyers, Jr.—Knoxville, Tennessee, first black to serve on the House Judiciary Committee (1966)

William Hastie—Knoxville, Tennessee, first black federal judge

John R. Lynch—a native of Mississippi, first black man to preside over a national convention of the Republican party

Ebenezer Bassett—born in Litchfield, Connecticut, first Black to represent the United States abroad

John M. Langston—Virginia, first Black elected to public office in the United States

GA1147

Map It!

Directions:

Match the name of each politician with the letter in his/her native state.

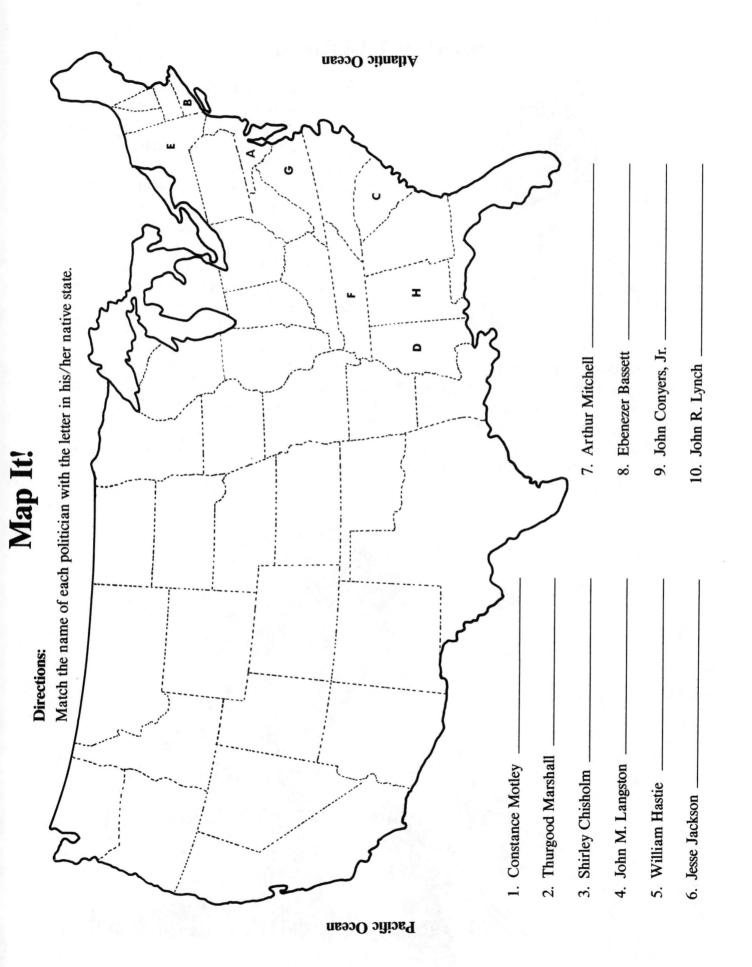

Atlantic Ocean

Pacific Ocean

1. Constance Motley _____
2. Thurgood Marshall _____
3. Shirley Chisholm _____
4. John M. Langston _____
5. William Hastie _____
6. Jesse Jackson _____

7. Arthur Mitchell _____
8. Ebenezer Bassett _____
9. John Conyers, Jr. _____
10. John R. Lynch _____

GA1147

Shirley Chisholm

Shirley Chisholm was born in 1924 in Brooklyn, New York. She and her mother moved to the island of Barbados in the West Indies where she lived from age three to age ten. When she was a young girl living in Barbados, her grandmother told her that she was something special and that she was going to accomplish many things. When she graduated from Columbia University in New York, she worked as a nursery school teacher and as a director of the child care center. In 1964 she was elected to the New York Assembly where she served for four years.

In 1968 she became the first black woman ever elected to the United States Congress. She served from 1969-1983 as a representative from Brooklyn, New York. In 1972 Chisholm campaigned to be the Democratic party nominee for President of the United States. She was not successful but she wrote a book, *The Good Fight*, which told the story of her campaign for the presidency. Later she wrote her autobiography, *Unbought and Unbossed*. In 1982 she decided not to run for reelection. She chose to write, to teach and to travel around the country giving lectures.

GA1147

Success Ladder

Directions:

Place the events of Shirley Chisholm's life on the right in the correct order on the ladder on the left.

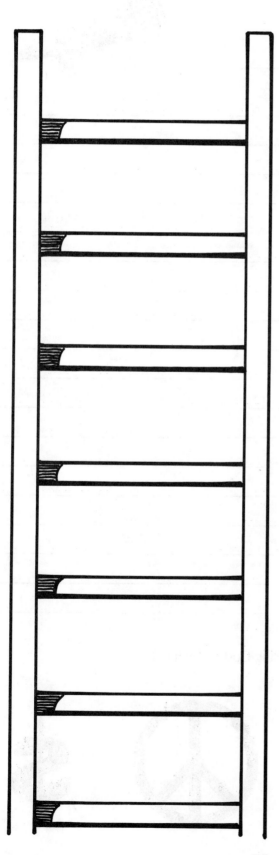

Wrote a Book

Elected to U.S. Congress

Campaigned for President of the U.S.

Born in 1924

Nursery School Teacher

Graduated from Columbia University

Elected to New York Assembly

Speaking Engagement

If you could travel to any country and speak on any subject, where would you go and what topic would you choose for your speech?

I would go to _____
(Country)

I would speak on _____
(Topic or Subject)

This is what I would say: _____

_____

_____

_____

_____

_____

_____

_____

_____

_____

_____

_____

_____

_____

_____

_____

_____

Some sample topics: Pollution, War, Peace, Rising Cost of Living, etc.

GA1147

Black Cowboys

Thousands of black men and women helped to explore and settle the West. Most of these Westerners were ex-slaves who had been freed after the Civil War. There were cowboys, hunters, trappers, mountain men, pony express riders, horse wranglers, cooks and trailblazers. They joined wagon trains, herded cattle or just headed West for the adventure. More than 5000 black cowboys rode the range from Texas to Montana. After the Civil War, *dangerous* wild cattle roamed the *plains*. Only the brave and skillful *cowboys* could *stalk* the wild animals. One such cowboy was Henry Beckwith, "The Coyote." He could sniff the air, find the cattle and bring them in for *branding*. He was called The Coyote because he worked alone usually at night. He was smart, tough and brave.

Bose Ikard was another skillful cowboy. He was born a slave in Mississippi and later moved to Texas. As a boy he could *rope, tie* and *brand* a *steer* as well as any grown man. When he was older, Bose *hired* out to Charles Goodnight, a famous cattle *rancher*. Bose helped to *herd* more than 2000 *cattle* north to Colorado. For the next four years, Bose and Goodnight became true and loyal friends. Once he saved Goodnight's life from a herd of *stampeding* cattle. Tales of Bose Ikard's *adventures* thrilled many young cowboys. They hoped someday to rope and *ride* like Bose Ikard. When Ikard died, Goodnight erected a *tombstone* on his grave with this inscription: "Served with me four years on the Goodnight-Loving *Trail*. Never shirked a duty or disobeyed an order. Rode with me in many *stampedes*; participated in three engagements with *Comanches*. Splendid behavior."

Bill Pickett was a *rodeo* rider. He was born in Texas. He rode ranches in South America as well as the United States. He became known as The Dusky Demon. He could catch a steer by its *horn* and make it fall to the ground by twisting its neck and biting into its upper lip. This is called *bulldogging*. Bill Pickett was the best of the bulldoggers. In fact, he invented it. This technique is still used in rodeo events today but without the biting. In 1907 Bill signed a contract with the famous 101 Ranch Wild West Show of Oklahoma. Bill Pickett became internationally famous for his rodeo *performances*. He made appearances in the United States, Canada, Mexico and Argentina. In 1914 he performed for King George and Queen Mary of England. He retired from the rodeo in 1916 and bought a ranch in Chandler, Oklahoma. In 1932 he was killed by an angry *stallion*. He was buried at White Base Monument, Maryland, Oklahoma.

Nat Love was a ranch *rider* with expert *marksmanship*. He was born in Tennessee. Love was hired by the Pete Gillinger Company of Arizona to herd cattle. At a Fourth of July *celebration*, after a cattle drive to Deadwood, South Dakota, Love participated in an open *contest* to rope, *throw*, tie, *saddle* and *mount* an untamed *bronco*. This he did in nine minutes! He also won a *shooting* contest with amazing accuracy. From that time forward, he was known as Deadwick Dick. In 1907 he wrote his autobiography, *The Life and Times of Nat Love, Better Known in Cattle Country as "Deadwood Dick."*

GA1147

Ring and Rope

Here are thirty-four words from Black Cowboys. Can you find them?

```
J Y S Y W O P I L T B H K T M V C T Z I I E W Q Q
F L R D E C S R S M Z J R L B Q J A H Q T N N R Z
P N R Q B L G K Q N L C C G O L B J K O H S J O A
J V X V G R K N D Q P Z U C S U V E R Y A E H E J
S Y B U L L D O G G I N G E S M K E G L G C Z P R D
R T G N I T O O H S H T Q L U E D U E Z P N L K D
C I A L U N R S G V S S S E O I L F X T H A X E O
Y I D M Q Z Y Z B L N E P B R C U D C A I M Q B N
O Y W E P O R R I I A T O R E L N I D N A R K O R
L I Y A B E P D D V M N J A G A E O S A S O N P O
Q F L W X G D R I B S O U T N T K V R I S F Q C H
G Q O D C Q R I F E K C L I A P O S L B L R S E J
M C T L H R X L N I R Q P O D A P M H I R E D I L
J H X V L P A Y E G A Q S N M L Q Z B N K P H C W
W Y R L K Z X M A P M E T T Z J K L K S Z R P J B
B T T K X S M V G D H G K R X Y A A G Y T B S C E
A D U H L F T E Q C V A H A F X X F L L I O A T L
K L A T S T Y A N U P E C I G N I D N A R B N T T
O E D O R N Y A L S W O N L N I W R C R K F J E T
N U Y O X U M X S L M N K T R W D F E O W M T H A
F W P D M O I S U R I M D E U U O N L H U G E B C
U E V F C M K G E I I O E R T R V R A L C N E V Z
R W S T A M P E D E S T N I E M E H H R T N T O T
G E Y K H K H A K R S O E G Z H V S G T B A A R X
F J J R E W A K Y Y L Z M F Y V H V W V X D K R Y
```

Here are the words to look for:

brand	stallion	mount
bronco	stampeding	plains
cattle	throw	ride
Comanches	tombstone	rodeo
dangerous	adventures	saddle
hired	branding	stalk
marksmanship	bulldogging	stampedes
performances	celebration	steer
rancher	contest	tie
rider	cowboys	trail
rope	herd	
shooting	horn	

68

Cowboy Memorials

Read the memorial written to Bose Ikard. Write a memorial for each cowboy's tombstone below. (Use information from Black Cowboys.) After you have finished, write the cowboy's famous nickname at the top of the tombstone.

1. Nat Love

2. Bill Pickett

3. Henry Beckwith

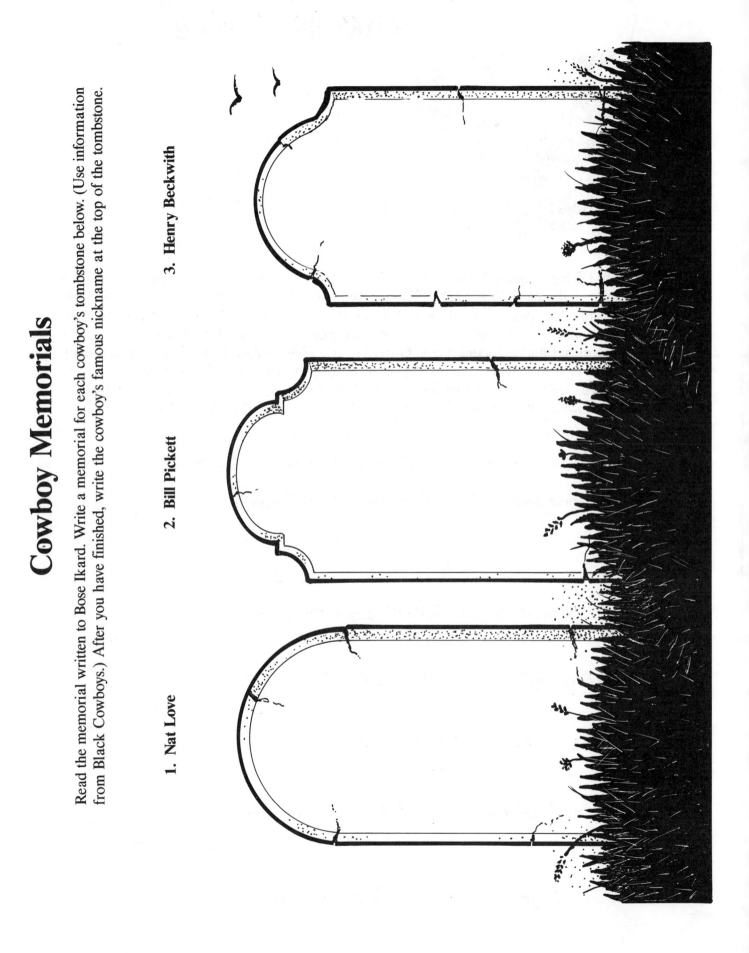

GA1147

Goodnight-Loving

Goodnight-Loving is not the name of a new rock or singing group. It was one of the major cattle trails in the early West. After the Civil War there was a great demand for beef in the North. There were many cattle trails and many cowboys who drove cattle along these trails. One of the most famous cattle trails was the Goodnight-Loving Trail. It was founded by two Texas cattlemen, Charles Goodnight and Oliver Loving. They combined a herd of Texas longhorns and set out to deliver them from Weatherford, Texas, to Bozeman, Montana. It was a long, hard trip. The trail passed through deserts, over mountains and through hostile Indian territory. Two black cowboys who herded cattle on the Goodnight-Loving Trail were Bose Ikard and Jim Fowler.

Trace over the Goodnight-Loving Trail on the map, then answer the questions below.

1. Name the states through which the Goodnight-Loving Trail passed.

    A. _____ B. _____ C. _____

    D. _____ E. _____

2. Name two black cowboys that rode the Goodnight-Loving Trail.

    _____ and _____

3. Name the state where the Goodnight-Loving Trail began.

    _____

4. Name the state where the Goodnight-Loving Trail ended.

    _____

5. Name the two Texas cattlemen who founded the Goodnight-Loving Trail.

    _____ and _____

6. Name two other famous cattle trails that helped to "open the West."

    _____ and _____

GA1147

The Goodnight-Loving Trail

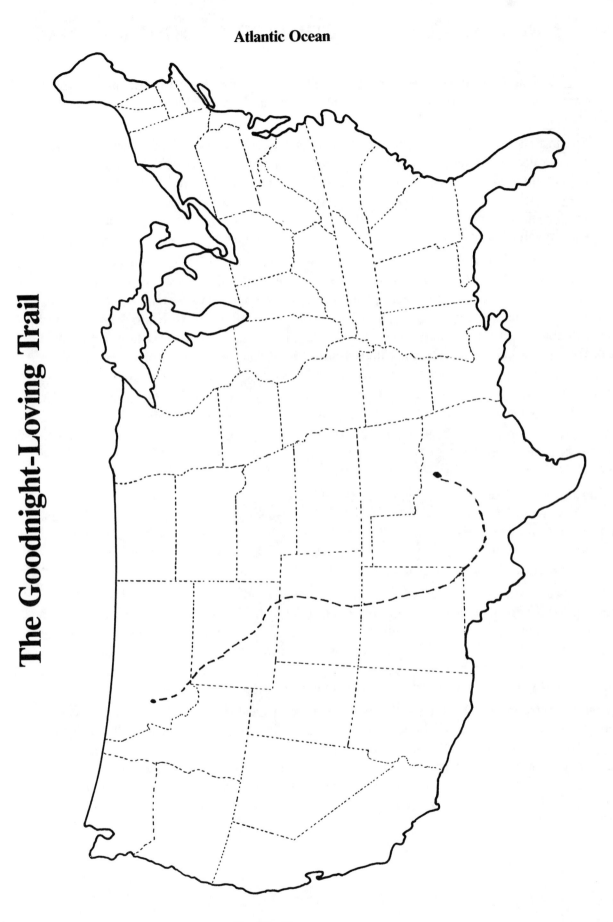

Atlantic Ocean

Pacific Ocean

71

GA1147

Black Pioneers, Pony Express and Mountain Men

For some black Americans, going West turned out to be quite profitable. Many became successful businessmen. Some set up motels, ran restaurants, stores and shops. Others became wealthy landowners.

One of the most successful businessmen was Alexander Leidesdorff. He migrated from the West Indies and operated as a ship captain between San Francisco and Hawaii. Leidesdorff saved his money and invested it wisely. He bought land and built the City Hotel in San Francisco. He became a civic and educational leader, member of the first city council, city treasurer, and the first elected city mayor. Leidesdorff died in 1848. He was only thirty-eight years old, but he left an estate valued at more than one and a half million dollars!

Hiram Young was an expert blacksmith. On his way West, he stopped in Independence, Missouri, to repair his wagon. He noticed that many other wagoners needed their wagons repaired, too. He gave his assistance. Many offered to pay for these much needed services. Hiram did not travel any further West. He opened up a blacksmith and wagon repair shop. By 1890 western travel had increased so much that he had to enlarge his shop and hire extra men. Hiram Young built many of the wagons that took many people to explore the West.

On January 27, 1860, the Russell, Major and Waddell Shipping Company announced that they would hire pony express riders to carry mail across the continent. This would be an extremely difficult task. The heavy snows in the mountains made riding extremely difficult. The Gosuite and Paiute Indian tribes of the Great Basin were on the warpath. Only the brave and determined were encouraged to apply for the job. Black riders George Munroe rode the Merced to Mariposa Route in California, and William Robinson rode the Stockton Route.

Biddy Mason was a black pioneer woman who became part of the westward movement. She was born a slave in Mississippi. Her master led a three-hundred-wagon caravan to California. Biddy's job was to watch the cattle and keep them close to the wagon. When they reached California, the laws there forbade slavery. Biddy settled in Los Angeles and became a wealthy landowner. She shared her wealth by donating land for churches and schools.

Mary Fields was born a slave in Tennessee in 1832. She escaped slavery and moved to Montana. She became an expert stage driver. Often she would drive through severe winter storms to deliver mail. For eight years she met every train to collect the mail. At the age of seventy-three she gave up the mail route and settled in Cascade, Montana. Mary died in 1914 at about the age of eighty-one. A picture of her sketched by a famous artist hangs in the Stockton Bank in Cascade. The courage that she displayed during her lifetime made her a legend in Montana.

Numerous black trappers and traders called mountain men blazed the western trails. Pierre Bonza worked for the American Fur Company. Edward Rose was hired by General William Ashley as interpreter of Indian languages. Once during an Indian attack he fought so courageously that he was granted the rank of ensign under Colonel Henry Leavenworth who had come to rescue Ashley's party. Edward Rose was buried on the Missouri River. Old steamboat maps still show his grave as a landmark. Moses Harris, Polite Laboss and James Beckwourth are other mountain men of this era.

Hats Off!

The hats of these famous pioneers have fallen off the hat tree. Can you place them where they belong? Place the letters of the hats that match the clues in the blanks.

1. _____ owned a blacksmith and wagon repair shop

2. _____ built the City Hotel in San Francisco

3. _____ rode the Merced-Mariposa pony express

4. _____ pioneer woman, wealthy landowner

5. _____ his name appears on old steamboat maps

6. _____ pioneer, woman stage driver

7. _____ expert trapper, worked for American Fur Company

8. _____ rode the Stockton pony express

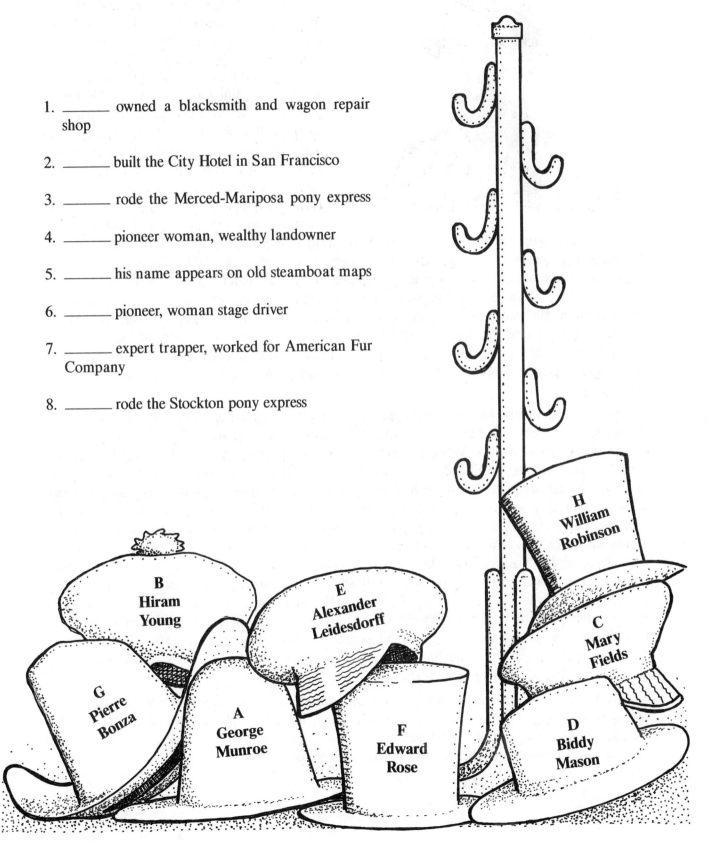

GA1147

James Beckwourth
(1798-1867)

One of the greatest mountain men of the West was James Beckwourth. He was born in *Virginia*. His mother was a slave. His father was the son of a wealthy plantation owner. When he was old enough, his father took him to a blacksmith in *St. Louis, Missouri,* to learn a trade but Jim had other ideas. He fought with his father and fled to the wilderness of southern *Illinois.* There he learned to hunt and trap. He became a hunter for the Illinois Mining Camp. This experience helped him to become an expert hunter, trapper and explorer. He took a boat to *New Orleans.* The Louisiana Territory was still unexplored but when he arrived he met with unkind treatment. He had heard that further west the color of one's skin did not matter much. It was strength and bravery that counted. In 1928 Jim learned that an expedition was about to leave for the Rocky Mountains. The expedition was sponsored by General William Ashley of the Rocky Mountain Fur Company. Jim returned to St. Louis and joined the expedition. He could trap even the most elusive animals and skin them for their fur. When the trip was completed, Jim had proved himself to be a very valuable member of the expedition. He had earned the respect and admiration of everyone. Once he attracted everyone's attention by leading a grizzly bear down Main Street, an animal that he had brought back from the mountains.

It was not long before Jim was asked to go on another expedition. This time he was asked to go into the Great Salt Lake Region of *Utah*. There he was to meet Bill Sublette, a captain trapper for General Ashley. When he arrived, Sublette proposed that Beckwourth help set up a trading post among the Blackfeet Indians. This was a dangerous undertaking but Jim agreed to do it. His tan appearance helped him move among the Indians without attracting too much attention. His stay was so successful that he married an Indian woman and settled there for a while. Later, he left the Blackfeet and lived among the Crow Indians for six years. There he became a great warrior and chief. After fifteen years, he returned to St. Louis and worked as a guide and interpreter. Once he went to *Florida* but soon returned to the West. He once bought a ranch and tried to settle down, but when he heard of the California Gold Rush, he abandoned the ranch and set out for *California*. He later bought a store in *Denver, Colorado*. Shortly afterwards, he was asked by the U.S. government to go on a peace mission to the Crow Indians. He was to ask them to remain at peace and not go on the warpath. The journey to the Crow Indians was long and hard. During this mission Jim became sick and died. He was buried by the Indians among their chiefs.

Jim Beckwourth, hunter, trapper, guide, interpreter among Indians, advisor to travelers, fur trader, was a man of many talents. He has earned a place in history. He discovered a pass through the Sierra Nevada Mountains. That pass is known as Beckwourth Pass. Beckwourth, California, and Beckwourth Peak are other places named in his honor.

GA1147

X Marks the Spot

Directions:

Place each italicized location from the story beside the correct "X" on the map. Then locate and mark the Rocky Mountains and the Sierra Nevada Mountains.

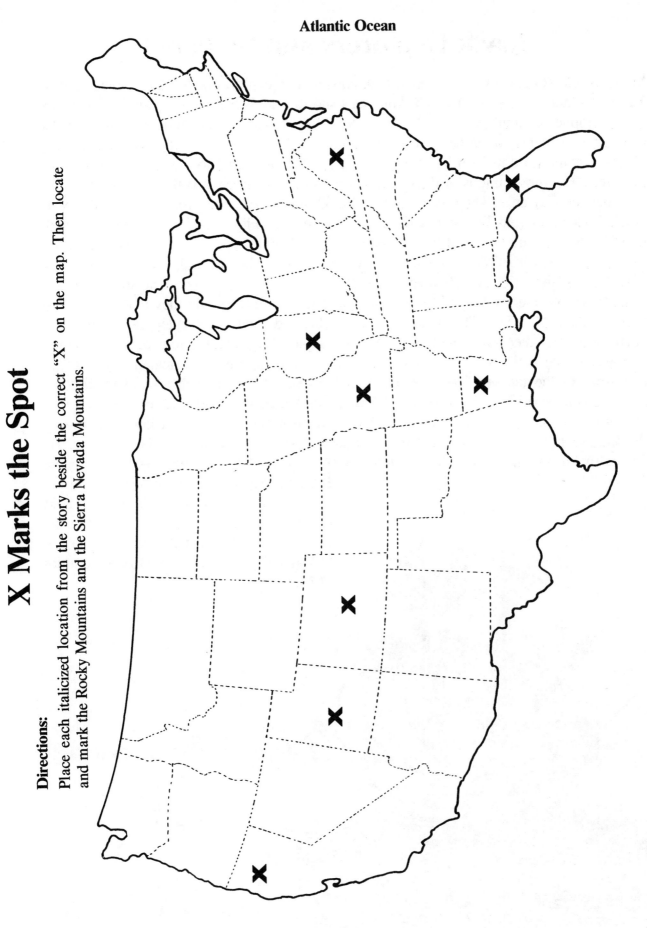

GA1147

Black Explorers and Settlers

Many black Americans helped in the discovery and exploration of the United States. The first black American to reach America's shores was Pedro Nino. He was a member of Christopher Columbus' team. In 1513 Nuflio de Olan and twenty-nine other Blacks traveled with Balboa when he discovered the Pacific Ocean. When Cortez reached Mexico, Blacks accompanied him on his trip. Many African slaves came to America with Spanish explorers. The most famous of these was Estevanico. Estevanico was the servant of Andre Dorantes de Carranze. They were among the 600-man expedition that came to the New World looking for gold. By the time the expedition reached Florida, only 400 men remained. In 1528 the crew had made it to Galveston, Texas. Only 80 men had survived starvation, Indians and weather. The survivors were taken as slaves by the Indians. After one year only four of the original 600 men were left. Estevanico was one of the four. For five years these four men wandered through jungles and swamps. Finally they reached Mexico City on July 24, 1536. The Mexican ruler welcomed them. The ruler had heard that north of his city there were gold, silver and gemstones. He asked the four men to continue to travel to see if this was true. The three other men refused but Estevanico was eager to go on. In the fall of 1538 Estevanico and a small band of men set out to discover cities of gold and silver. Each band of Indians that they met told tales of "Seven Cities of Cibola" to the north. In May of 1539 Estevanico looked over into a land which only the Indians had looked upon. Estevanico had led the group to present-day Arizona. As he approached what looked like to him "Seven Cities of Gold," he was killed by the Indians. The life of this brave and daring adventurer was ended. To this day no gold was found, but the people of the southwestern United States still tell the tales of a black "Mexican" who gave his life to see the states of Mexico and Arizona.

GA1147

An Estevanico Interview

You are Estevanico. You have been asked to appear on the *Donnie King Live* TV program to talk about your adventures as an explorer. Prepare yourself for the interview by answering the following questions. When you are finished, ask classmates to interview you.

1. What is your name? _____

2. Why did you come to the New World? _____

3. How many men were on the first expedition to the New World? _____

4. How many men had survived when you reached Florida? _____
   Galveston, Texas? _____

5. How many men were with you when you reached Mexico City? _____

6. When did you reach Mexico City? _____

7. What did the Mexican ruler request of you? _____

8. How did the other men feel about the request? _____

9. How did you feel about the request? _____

10. Did you find gold? _____ What present day state did you
    find? _____

GA1147

Jean Baptiste Pointe Du Sable

The city of Chicago, Illinois, was founded by a black man from Haiti. Chicago is the second largest city in the United States. Jean Baptiste Pointe du Sable was born in St. Marc, *Haiti*, in 1745. He was the son of a rich French merchant who had married a slave in Haiti. Du Sable was sent to *France* for his education. In 1765 his father sent him to *New Orleans* to seek new business for the family company. When the Spanish took control of New Orleans, Du Sable left for St. Louis, another area controlled by France. He set up a thriving business with the Indians. In 1767 the British took St. Louis and Du Sable moved to present-day Peoria, Illinois. Here he lived among the Potawatomi Indians. He married an Indian woman and became familiar with Pontiac, the great Indian chief. In 1769 Du Sable went to *Canada*. During his travel between Peoria and Canada, he stopped at a place called *Eschikago* by the Indians. In 1772 he decided to build a trading post in this place. In 1774 he finished the post and brought his family and Indians to Eschikago. It was here that *Chicago* was first settled. Du Sable's little settlement continued to grow. He built a poultry house, a dairy, a bake house and several additional buildings. He developed a thriving trading business with Indians and trappers. It was a convenient place to trade.

After the Revolutionary War the government sent out agents to survey land and sell it to settlers. Du Sable had no title to show ownership of his little community. He sold most of his belongings and moved to St. Charles, *Missouri*. Jean Baptiste du Sable died on August 28, 1818, at the age of seventy-three. He was buried in an unmarked grave in St. Boremeo Cemetery. On October 25, 1968, the state of Illinois and the city of Chicago held a ceremony and placed a granite stone on Du Sable's grave honoring him as the founder of one of the world's largest cities, Chicago.

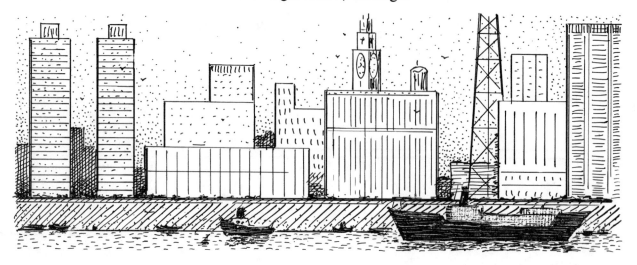

GA1147

Information, Please!

Fold two sheets of notebook paper in half to measure 8½″ x 5½″.

Staple the sheets together to make a booklet of four pages. Research information about the places in italics in the story of Jean Baptiste Pointe du Sable, and write the information in your booklet. Make the cover of your booklet interesting and colorful.

GA1147

Benjamin "Pap" Singleton
(1809-1892)

In August of 1882 in Topeka, Kansas, a Grand Complimentary Anniversary Celebration was given in honor of Benjamin "Pap" Singleton. It was one of the biggest celebrations ever given to honor a black person. The celebration included a twenty-two-gun salute and speeches by the governor of Kansas and the mayor of Topeka.

After the Civil War, many white former slave owners were angry. They had not wanted their slaves to go free, and they would not hire an ex-slave. Therefore many black, ex-slaves found it hard to find work so that they could make a decent living for their families. Benjamin Singleton wanted to find a place for his people. In 1873 he traveled to the state of Kansas. He found it a good place to begin a new life. He had a plan. His plan was to bring ex-slaves to Kansas so that they might find jobs. The state officials of Kansas listened to his plan. They promised to help Blacks who would come to Kansas. "Pap" Singleton returned to the South and led more than 300 black families to Kansas. They founded Singleton Colony, near Baxter Springs in Cherokee County. In the years to follow thousands of Blacks came to Kansas. They settled there and established communities such as Nicodemus, Morton, Dunlap, Mudtown and Rattlebone Hollow.

You Are Invited

Pretend that you lived during "Pap" Singleton's time. Design an invitation to invite people to attend the Grand Complimentary Anniversary Celebration.

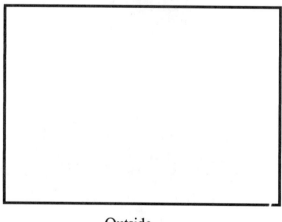

Outside

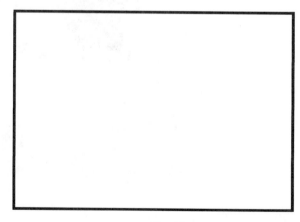

Inside

Create a radio or TV ad announcing the celebration.

GA1147

George Bush

George Bush was born in the state of Missouri in 1791. His parents were servants for a wealthy fur trading family. In 1814 a war for control of New Orleans broke out between the United States and Great Britain. Bush fought in the war under Major Andrew Jackson. After the war, George joined the Hudson Bay Fur Company and traveled to the Pacific Coast to buy furs. George loved the Pacific Coast territory and vowed someday to return to live there.

In 1843 when he had saved over two thousand dollars, he led his family and seven white men and their families on a wagon train. They traveled over the Oregon Trail to the Columbia River Valley. Because he was black, he was not allowed to settle in the first territory that he reached. He and his train continued across the Oregon border to the tip of Puget Sound. There he set up a grist and lumber mill powered by an eighty-foot waterfall. They were the first Americans to settle at Puget Sound. He named the new settlement New Market which was later called Tumwater. It was because of this settlement that the United States claimed land south of the forty-ninth parallel, where the boundary of the United States and Canada lies.

The Bush family became wealthy. One of his sons raised a prized wheat crop. A sample of this crop can be seen at the Smithsonian Institute in Washington, D.C. Bush died in 1867, but his son William Owens became a leader after his father. He became an influential member of the Washington State Legislature.

GA1147

Bush Boggles

Complete the statements using information from the Bush story.

1. George Bush was born in the state of ___ ___ ___ ___ ___ ⃝ ___ ___

2. Bush fought in the war between the U.S. and Great Britain under Major ___ ⃝ ___ ___ ⃝ ___ ___ ___ ___ ___ ___ ___ ⃝ ___ ___ ___

3. Bush worked for the ___ ⃝ ⃝ ___ ⃝ ___ ___ ___ ___ ___ ___ Fur Company.

4. Bush's wagon train traveled over the old ___ ___ ___ ⃝ ___ ___ ___ ⃝ ___ ___ ___ ___

5. Bush loved the ⃝ ___ ___ ___ ___ ___ ___ Coast territory.

Unscramble the circled letters to find the hidden word to complete this statement.

Bush and his family were the first Americans to settle at ___ ___ ___ ___ ___ ___ ___ ___ ___ ___

Other Explorers

In January of 1803 William Clark and Meriwether Lewis were sent by President Thomas Jefferson to explore the Louisiana Territory. With them was York, a black servant who was of great service during the two-year expedition. He helped to keep the Lewis and Clark Expedition team alive by performing feats of strength for the Indians in exchange for food.

Jacob Dodson was a volunteer member of the exploring team of John C. Frémont, "The Pathfinder."

Dodson participated in the "Bear Flag" revolt against Mexico to make California a part of the United States. He was with Frémont on one of the most famous rides in United States history—the ride from Los Angeles to Monterey, California, to warn General Stephen Kearny of an uprising against the Americans. It is said that they traveled over 840 miles in eight days!

When Dodson first joined Frémont on expeditions, he was only eighteen years old, but Frémont journals and reports frequently mentioned the loyalty and service of this brave young man.

GA1147

Circular Explorers

Follow the circle to find the names of two black explorers and three expedition leaders. Use the names that you find to complete the statements below.

Begin here.

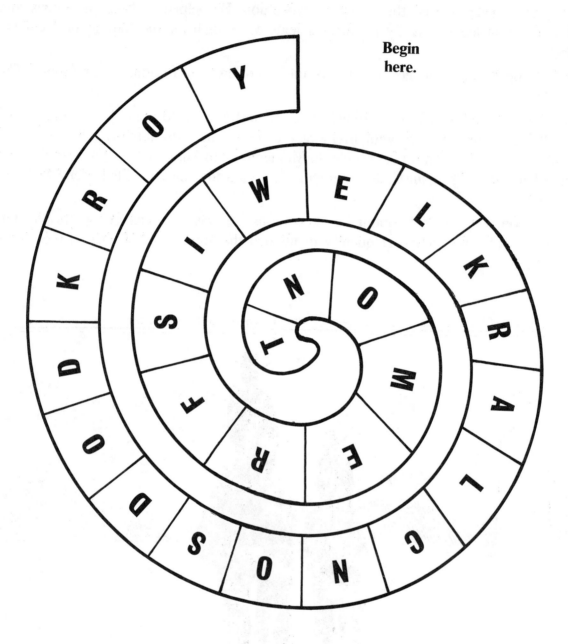

1. They were sent by President Thomas Jefferson to explore the Louisiana Territory. _____ and _____

2. He helped to keep the expedition team alive by performing feats of strength in exchange for food. _____

3. He participated in the "Bear Flag" revolt against Mexico. _____

4. He was called The Pathfinder. _____

Scrambled Explorers

Directions:

Unscramble the name in each ship to match the spaces on the left. Then unscramble the circled letters to find the name of a famous black settler.

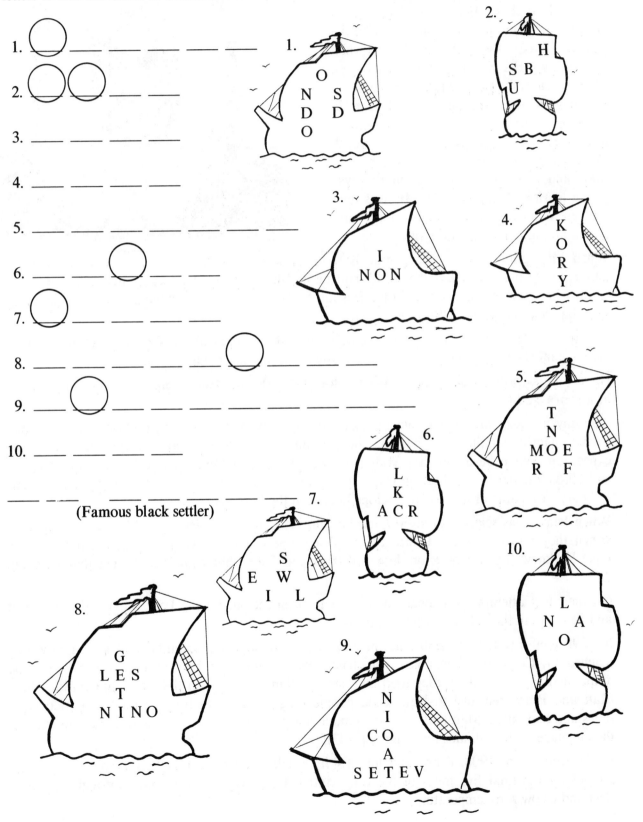

1. ◯ __ __ __ __ __ __

2. ◯◯ __ __ __ __

3. __ __ __ __ __

4. __ __ __ __

5. __ __ __ __ __

6. __ __ ◯ __ __ __

7. ◯ __ __ __ __

8. __ __ __ __ ◯ __ __ __

9. __ ◯ __ __ __ __ __ __

10. __ __ __ __ __

__ __ __ __ __ __ __ __ __
(Famous black settler)

85

Matthew Henson
(1866-1955)

Matt Henson was the first man to set foot on the North Pole. Henson was born on a farm in Maryland in 1866, one year after the ending of the Civil War. His mother died when he was two. His father died six years later. At the age of eleven Matt ran away to Washington, D.C. He spent several years in Washington as a dishwasher. Matt became restless. He wanted to see more of the world. He traveled to Baltimore, Maryland. In Maryland, he worked aboard a ship that was to sail to Hong Kong in China. He was only thirteen years old. The captain of the ship taught him how to read and write.

When Matt grew to be a young man he had learned much from his travel and reading. He had sailed to many parts of the world, and he had learned about many groups of people. One entire winter the ship was frozen in the Russian harbor due to icy conditions. When spring came, Matt had learned to speak Russian fluently.

One day while sailing from Jamaica to Baltimore, the captain of the ship died. Matt was now alone again. The captain had taught Matt many things about life and people.

He left the ship and went back to Washington, D.C. He was twenty-one years old and worked at a men's clothing store.

One day a young man came into the store to buy a helmet. The man told Matt that he was a civil engineer for the Navy and that he was on his way to Central America on a surveying expedition. When he found that Matt had already been to Central America and other places as well, he offered to hire Matt to travel with him. The man who bought the helmet was Robert E. Peary. A lifetime of friendship developed between the two men.

When Peary was selected to go to Greenland to study the polar ice caps, Matt went with him. When they returned to the United States, Peary knew that he would try to reach the North Pole. He knew that many before him had tried and failed, but with Matt he felt that he could do it.

On their first attempt, an expedition crew of thirteen set out for the Pole. After one year, Matt and Peary were the only two who remained.

In 1898 they traveled over 250 miles in deep snowdrifts and over mountains of ice. Finally they reached Ft. Congress. Then misfortune struck. Peary's toes had become frozen and had to be amputated. Again in 1904, they tried and came within 175 miles of the top of the world. When Matt and Peary returned to New York, people laughed at them because they had tried eight times and had failed. Matt had learned so much about Arctic winds and weather. He had learned the language of the Eskimos and their way of life.

In the summer of 1908, Peary and four Eskimos left other crew members at base camp and set out for the final five miles of the trip. Matt led the way. They traveled through blizzards, sleet and below zero temperatures.

On April 6, 1909, they arrived 90 degrees north. Matt checked his instrument and sure enough, Matt had reached the North Pole. Peary arrived forty-five minutes later with Eskimos and a team of dogs. At last, after eighteen years—a dream had been fulfilled. Matt planted the American flag and Peary saluted it.

Peary died twelve years later but Matt lived to be eighty-eight years old. He died in 1955. He was buried in Woodlawn Cemetery in New York City.

In 1954 President Eisenhower honored Matt at the White House. In 1961 the state of Maryland passed a bill to place a bronze plaque in the state house to honor Matt Henson. In April of 1988, seventy-nine years after Matt Henson planted the American flag at the North Pole, his remains and those of his wife were brought from New York and placed in Arlington National Cemetery beside Admiral Robert E. Peary. Above them a granite headstone bears this inscription: "The lure of the Arctic is tugging at my heart, to me the trail is calling, the old trail, the trail that is always new." Matt's American-Eskimo descendants attended the burial ceremony which included full military honors. Matt Henson had finally been given the honor that he deserved for his bravery and leadership in being the first to stand at the North Pole.

GA1147

Icy Adventure

Directions:

Can you climb to the North Pole?

Answer the questions correctly and in order. Each time you answer a question correctly give yourself 10 points and move up to the next level. You must have 100 points to reach the North Pole.

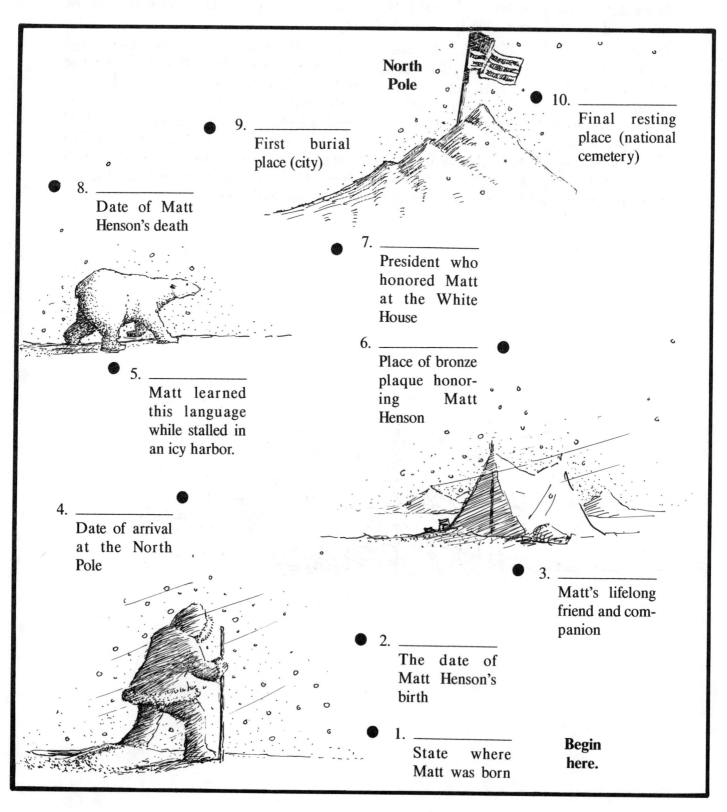

North Pole

10. _____
Final resting place (national cemetery)

9. _____
First burial place (city)

8. _____
Date of Matt Henson's death

7. _____
President who honored Matt at the White House

6. _____
Place of bronze plaque honoring Matt Henson

5. _____
Matt learned this language while stalled in an icy harbor.

4. _____
Date of arrival at the North Pole

3. _____
Matt's lifelong friend and companion

2. _____
The date of Matt Henson's birth

1. _____
State where Matt was born

Begin here.

88

Answer Key

Woodson's Puzzle, Page 2

1. Berea
2. twenty-two
3. Carter
4. coal
5. year
6. Sorbonne
7. Black
8. Canton
9. Harvard
10. on
11. life
12. February

Two important words: Black History

Native States, Page 7

Evidence, Page 11

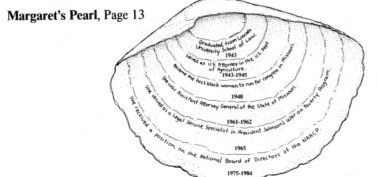

```
I H A O Q M V U P A M V Y I G Q Y W E A A T L I H
H N I A T S R K B V H T K H O R F Q S C E P D N P
B T A I Q L A V H H P K O P W Y T N V V X J O W L
R O D O J M N X C L W S O D T T Q T Y Q L S U X R
K J I O O A W G L M U H W E E M X Y R T D P P C I
O A A O X D V A O M T O O A W K A P Y R A I Q W N
E R R T F H G E L O N R K V U P C L A A S Z Q A Z
C E M Q O T L B U D E R J A X Z H L H A A J Q H
G L I C E X K L H E S J B N S C L B A U K K R U
A X P I G D O C N O M N J F Z J U H W Z F O
E E F C O Q L A O V I X Z T R T M B M B T S H Q I
F U G W R P X N P B H C S X I W F Q X Q W R S J
U Y L N L E O I T B U Q V Y M Q W Q N V N C A S
D Z N J L S J U R G H W J S E S H N I X Q S H W M
R U R A R V U H Y A Z Y R F G Z E G K L U W S Z N
A I O A S S F V S V T U E P W G J Q N O S M U O J
W F P I B H T T C V B H E D K G L A P V R O S X U
O R K V Q H I C O R L E X C Q Z U M E Y N N U
H D X E A E T Q V D Q K U J A X U P Q C I R S K R
M Q V W C O C V U W B Y V B N I M C I B Q N N U P
Y J R N F E D F R C L I W D A D Y X O B Z W T I L
S Y N O M E L C N Q E I W A F N U R L U G M I N G
G B A E M L I X Y G W W C A G B G F I O O B W G I
M O U J V E K P C D M N M K H F S S V F L H C R A
P V U A W P F C Y U E Q C I U O Y W L B O Y I V A
```

Margaret's Pearl, Page 13

Clemon's Lemonade, Page 15

1968—Graduated with honors from Columbia Law School
1974—First Black to be elected to the Alabama Senate
1980—Appointed first black federal judge in the state of Alabama

Sojourner's Truth, Page 18

1. ✓ (true)
2. x (false)
3. x (false)
4. ✓ (true)
5. x (false)

Harriet Tubman, Page 19

Harriet Tubman was a conductor on the Underground Railroad.

Washington/Du Bois Circles, Page 23

Washington

1. Born in 1856
2. Believed that Blacks should learn a vocation or trade
3. Had a postage stamp issued in his honor
4. Founded Tuskegee Institute
5. Elected to the Hall of Fame at New York University

Du Bois

1. Born in 1868
2. Organized the NAACP
3. Believed in the "talented tenth"
4. Graduated from Harvard with a Ph.D. degree
5. Died in 1963 at the age of 95

Both Leaders

1. Received help from friends and neighbors to attend school
2. Came from a poor family
3. Wanted to help Blacks to have a better way of life
4. Was well-educated
5. Was a great leader

Escape! Page 24

1. Booker T. Washington
2. conductors
3. abolitionists
4. Harriet Tubman
5. W.E.B. Du Bois
6. George Washington Carver
7. Underground Railroad
8. David Walker
9. Sojourner Truth
10. Frederick Douglass

Role Play, Page 26

1. Refused to give up her seat on a city bus (started the Civil Rights Movement)
2. Organized this to use peaceful means of making changes
3. Won by Dr. King in 1964
4. Organized this to end bus segregation
5. Where Dr. Kiing was pastor at the beginning of the Civil Rights Movement

GA1147

Find It! Page 28

```
D Q K U J A X U P Q C R S K R R M Q V W C O C V U
W B Y V B N C I M C I Q N N U E P Y J R N F E D F
R C L I W D I A D Y X B Z W T T I L S Y N Q E I W
A F N U L U T Y T I N A M U H S G G B A E M L I X
Y G W W C A A G B G F I O O B I W G I M O U J V E
K P C D N M R N K H F S S V F N L H C R A P V U A
W P F C Y U C E Q C I U O Y W I L B O Y I V A H P
K H L Z Y C O D F Y C H B B K M N F F L V U M W X
J N N T J S M C H K M D S F T I H R L R K P F M F
A U W I Z S E L H G D K A M Y B B H P L S L E G T
B V B B T A D W M K S G T K K V W R X T V D Q U E
Y P E P P H C O W Z Y L P I K V O M O V E Q R K L
E Z O N B E L D C K O U T V P A M I W I L X J V L
H A A N V P J P O F S N Z H U X R O M G U E Z O I
E L P O E P R K U H N Z O R G A N I Z A T I O N V
E Z Z P W Y V Q R T C U F V V H M E A R R Z Z N
Q V Q U R K X T A P F A R V R R L R I A Q M O E
H E M D N W P A G K W O V Q F I V Q Z F I E L F E
I R J T E B T G E H A E A T X J O I T S N T Y P R
K N G N K C A O O W X V N R G W E L T P B T E X G
L D J Q C B Z I U C O A L I T I O N E M O A J E W
J L H K Q C E B S S K F M X T H N T Q N W X N C H
H T A E R G T I M E F S R P U V E X E X C V C U A
B S V O R W D C B F X U W A F I T Z X K M E H H Y
T Y Y L U W F B J U M C S F J E Q I N B B S E A S
```

1. *Time*
2. organization, PUSH
3. Democratic
4. Run
5. minister
6. Rainbow Coalition
7. Greenville
8. courageous, great
9. People, Humanity
10. riots, violence

Footsteps of the Past, Page 31

1. first clock 1761
2. corn planter 1834
3. electric light bulb filament 1882
4. railway telegraph 1887
5. shoe-lasting machine 1891
6. lubrication for steam engine 1892
7. a device to automatically join railroad cars when they bump 1897
8. golf tee 1899
9. gas mask 1912
10. traffic light 1923

Decoding, Page 32

1. Frederick Jones
2. Marvin Steward
3. Howard Jones
4. Donald Jefferson
5. T.J. Marshall
6. C.J. Walker
7. Rufus Stokes
8. Otis Boykins
9. Meredith Gourdine
10. Vance Marchbanks

Greetings, Page 34

1. Mr. Brown
2. Mr. Certain
3. Mr. Winters
4. Mr. Johnson
5. Mr. Miles

Thank You, Page 35

Dear Mr. Burr,
Thank you for inventing a device that helps to keep grass from clogging the lawn mower gears.

Dear Mr. Downing,
Thank you for inventing the big, blue mailbox.

Dear Mr. Lee,
Thank you for inventing the kneading machine.

Dear Mr. Purvis,
Thank you for inventing the fountain pen.

Dear Mr. Sampson,
Thank you for inventing a version of the clothes dryer.

Bookshelf, Page 40

1. Lorraine Hansberry, 1959
2. Gwendolyn Brooks, 1950
3. James Baldwin, 1953
4. Phillis Wheatley, 1773
5. Maya Angelou, 1970
6. Nikki Giovanni, 1968
7. Arna Bontemps, 1931
8. Alex Haley, 1976
9. Mildred Taylor, 1976
10. Paul Laurence Dunbar, 1896
11. Douglas Ward Turner, 1965-1966
12. Langston Hughes, 1956

Annual Great Writers' Awards, Page 42

Books and Novels
Imamu Baraka
James Emanuel
Clarence Major
Margaret Walker

Short Stories
Imamu Baraka
Nikki Giovanni
Bobb Hamilton

Songs and Plays
Imamu Baraka
Mae Jackson
Norman Jordan

Editors
Quandra Prettyman
Larry Thompson
Bobb Hamilton

Poetry
Imamu Baraka
Victor Cruz
Julia Fields
Marie Evans
Nikki Giovanni
Bobb Hamilton
Norman Jordan
William MacLean, Jr.
Clarence Major
Sonia Sanchez
Larry Thompson

GA1147

Whose Hands? Page 48

1. B	4. D
2. C	5. E
3. A	Mystery Sculptor: Richard Hunt

Complete It! Page 51

1. Charles Alston, E. Simms Campbell
2. Henry O. Tanner
3. Charles White
4. E. Simms Campbell
5. William Harper
6. Melvin Johnson
7. Edward Bannister
8. Charles Alston
9. Aaron Douglas
10. Robert Duncanson

Medical Time Tunnel, Page 54

1833—The first hospital for black patients was established.
1837—James McCune Smith became the first black doctor to earn a medical degree in the United States.
1876—Two major medical schools for Blacks were established.
1891—Provident Hospital in Chicago was founded.
1926—Dr. Ulysses Grant Dailey set up his own hospital.
1929—Dr. Theodore Lawless won the Harmon Award for Outstanding Achievement in Medicine

Official Scientists, Page 56

Physicist
Shirley Jackson
Walter Massey

Cancer Research
Jewel Cobb
Jane Wright

Biologist
Ernest Just

Math
David Blackwell

Chemistry
Lloyd Ferguson
Percy Julian

Transplant Physician
Samuel Kountz

Blood Bank
Charles Drew

Medical Teacher
W. Montague Cobb

Chemical Research and College President
Reatha Clark King

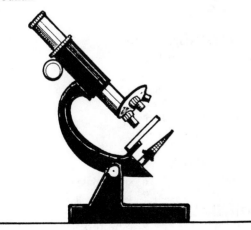

Challenger Time Line, Page 58

1942—Guion Bluford was born.
1964—Guion graduated from Penn State.
1965—He received his wings and became a pilot.
1972—Guion graduated from the Air Force Institute of Technology.
1978—Bluford received his Ph.D. degree in aerospace engineering.
1983—Guion became the first Black to fly in space.

Let's Take a Poll, Page 61

	1	2	3	4	5	6	7	8
Alabama	▓	▓	▓					
Florida	▓							
Georgia	▓							
Louisiana	▓							
Mississippi	▓	▓	▓					
North Carolina	▓	▓	▓					
South Carolina	▓	▓	▓	▓	▓	▓	▓	▓
Virginia	▓							

Map It! Page 63

1. B	6. C
2. A	7. H
3. E	8. B
4. G	9. F
5. F	10. D

Success Ladder, Page 65

1. Born in 1924
2. Graduated from Columbia University
3. Nursery School Teacher
4. Elected to New York Assembly
5. Elected to U.S. Congress
6. Campaigned for President of the U.S.
7. Wrote a Book

GA1147

Ring and Rope, Page 68

```
J Y S Y W O P I L T B H K T M V C T Z I I E W Q Q
F L R D E C S R S M Z J R L B Q J A H Q T N N R Z
P N R Q B L G K Q N L C C G O L B J K O H S J O A
J V X V G R K N D Q P Z U C S U V E R Y A E H E J
S V B U L L D O G G I N G E S M K E G L G C Z P R
R T G N I T O O H S H T Q L U E D U E Z P N L K D
C I A L U N R S G V S S S E O N L F X T H A X E O
Y I D M O Z Y Z B L N E P B R C U D C A I M Q B N
O Y W E P O R R I I A T O R E L N I D N A R K O R
L I Y A B E P D D V M N J A G A E O S A S O N P O
Q F L W X G D I B S O U T N T K V R S F Q C H H
G Q O D C Q R I F E K C L I A P O S L B L R S E J
M C T L H R X L N I R Q P O D A P M H I R E D I L
J H X V L P A Y E G A Q S N M L Q Z B N K P H C W
W Y R L K Z X M A P M E T T Z J K L K S Z R P J B
B T T K X S M V G D H G K R X Y A A G Y T B S C E
A D U H L F T E Q C V A H A F X X F L L O A T L
K L A T S T Y A N U P E C I G N I D R A R B N T T
O E D O R N Y A L S W O N U N I W R C R K F J E T
N U Y O X U M X S L M N K T R W D F E O W M T H A
F W P D M O I S U R I M D E U U O N L H U G E B C
U E V F C M K G E I O E R T R V R A L C N E V Z
R W S T A M P E D E S T N M E M E H H R T N T O T
G E Y K H K H A K R S O E G Z H V S G T B A A R X
F J J R E W A K Y Y L Z M F Y V H V W V X D K R Y
```

Cowboy Memorials, Page 69

1. Deadwood Dick
2. The Dusky Demon
3. The Coyote

Goodnight-Loving, Page 70

1. A. Texas   D. Wyoming
   B. New Mexico E. Montana
   C. Colorado
2. Bose Ikard and Jim Fowler
3. Texas
4. Montana
5. Charles Goodnight and Oliver Loving
6. Answers will vary.

Hats Off! Page 73

1. B   5. F
2. E   6. C
3. A   7. G
4. D   8. H

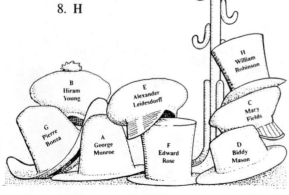

X Marks the Spot, Page 75

1. Virginia   5. Utah
2. St. Louis, Missouri 6. Florida
3. Southern Illinois   7. California
4. New Orleans, Louisiana 8. Denver, Colorado

An Estevanico Interview, Page 77

1. Estevanico
2. to search for gold
3. 600
4. 400, 80
5. 3
6. July 24, 1536
7. to continue to travel to search for gold
8. They refused.
9. I was eager to go on.
10. no, Arizona

Bush Boggles, Page 82

1. Missouri   4. Oregon Trail
2. Andrew Jackson   5. Pacific
3. Hudson Bay   Puget Sound

Circular Explorers, Page 84

Names in the circle are York, Dodson, Clark, Lewis and Frémont.

1. Lewis, Clark
2. York
3. Jacob Dodson
4. John C. Frémont

Scrambled Explorers, Page 85

1. Dodson   6. Clark
2. Bush   7. Lewis
3. Nino   8. Singleton
4. York   9. Estevanico
5. Frémont   10. Olan

Famous black settler: Du Sable

Icy Adventure, Page 88

1. Maryland   6. state house (Maryland)
2. 1866   7. Eisenhower
3. Robert E. Peary   8. 1955
4. April 6, 1909   9. New York City
5. Russian   10. Arlington

GA1147